THE SHERIFF OF CARLIN COUNTY

Roger L. Fields

Copyright © 2024 Roger L. Fields

All rights reserved.

No part of this book may be reproduced, stored in a retrieval system, or transmitted by any means, electronic, mechanical, photocopying, recording, or otherwise, without written permission from the author.

ISBN (Paperback): 979-8-9919700-4-4
ISBN (eBook): 979-8-9919700-3-7

Dedicated to the generations of Cherokees who endured hardships and tragedy, but by diligence and the strength of their character, continued our rich and unique culture.

I have always admired and respected the achievements of William Penn Adair Rogers, a fellow Oklahoman and Cherokee Nation citizen. Although I chose to use the name Will Rogers for the main character of this story, this is a work of fiction and is not intended to depict any events from the life of William Penn Adair Rogers.

Chapter One

Monday, May 27th, 2013, was my first day on the job as the interim Carlin County Sheriff. It had been an uneventful day and I was feeling comfortable in the role. My deputies had spent the day dealing with a handful of traffic issues from various parts of the county, but nothing significant had occurred. I had even allowed myself to think that maybe this job was not going to be too difficult for me. Just as I was closing my office door to leave for the evening, Deputy Watts, one of the deputies scheduled for the overnight shift, called Beverly, our office manager, and stated he had a family emergency and would not be able to patrol that evening.

I looked over at her and asked, "How did Sheriff Joe manage a situation like this?"

"Normally, if no deputies were available to cover the shift, Sheriff Joe would hold over for the evening and into the night. As soon as another deputy became available, they would make relief and the sheriff would go home. I will call and see if anybody can cover the shift."

"Thanks, Beverly," I replied.

Not wanting to inconvenience any of my deputies and trying to avoid paying more overtime than I had to, I knew I would need to cover part of the shift. "I will cover shift this evening, but have the Dispatcher let me know who is coming on shift and what time they can make relief."

It was a hot day for late May, and although a tall glass of iced tea would have been refreshing, I knew I was going to need a cup of coffee to keep me alert. An hour or so into my evening shift, I was en route to the Bar K convenience store to get a cup when an excited Dispatcher anxiously announced a crime in progress. Her voice echoed through the radio as she nervously announced, "All available units respond to a possible robbery at Grand Package Liquor on West Main Street."

I replied, "I am only a couple of miles away and will be there in two minutes."

The Dispatcher announced, "A person passing by the store called in and reported they thought a robbery was in progress."

Deputy Allen replied, "I am about ten minutes away and am en route."

The Sheriff of Carlin County

I felt a sense of irony that I was now responding to a possible crime in the patrol car that I once dreaded seeing driving up the road toward my house. I turned on my red and blue lights and siren. I quickly accelerated. As vehicles began pulling to the shoulder of the road to allow me to pass, the sound of the siren and the lights reflecting off cars and buildings, the rush of adrenaline hit me. I realized I was alone and didn't know what I would be walking into. I could feel my heart rate quicken. I was about to get my first law enforcement experience.

I raced my patrol car to the alley behind the store, parked about one-half block away, and jogged to the store.

With radio in hand, I announced, "I am at Grand Package Liquor."

"Has city police been notified?" I asked.

The Dispatcher responded, "No, but I will notify them now."

I glanced around the corner of the building and could see a small blue sedan parked outside the front door. I noticed Charlie's Burger Barn across the street had several cars parked in the parking lot. I was concerned about stray bullets if this turned ugly. I told myself to remember the crowd at Charlie's. I decided to gain entry through the back door and hoped it might be open. I was surprised but pleased the back door was not locked and was slightly ajar.

I notified dispatch, "I am making entry through the back door."

I slowly opened the door and crept into a back storage room. To the left, the room was littered with piles of broken-down boxes and trash to be removed. To the right, several cardboard boxes of future inventory were organized in tidy stacks. With the back door being unlocked and ajar, I assumed a store employee was in the process of carrying out the trash and was interrupted. Fortunately, there was a narrow path between the trash and the boxes of liquor leading to a doorway and out to the floor of the store. I noted a couple of shelves lining the wall adjacent to the doorway to my right. The shelves were overflowing with routine items such as bags, old signage, liquor posters, and cash register tape. Not surprisingly, an aroma of alcohol scented the air.

I could clearly hear two male voices; one voicing commands, and one desperate voice pleading with the other person to not shoot. I crept along the narrow pathway between the boxes as I made my way toward the doorway leading into the store. I paused momentarily beside the shelves. From this point, I could see the face of the cashier. He was probably in his forties with a medium build and dark brown hair that was beginning to reveal gray highlights on the sides. I could only see the back side of the robber but observed some physical characteristics of him as well. His head was covered with a black-knit ski mask. He was wearing blue sterile gloves like a doctor or nurse would wear while treating a patient. He was a slender man, maybe five feet ten inches to six feet tall. He may have weighed one-hundred and seventy-five pounds. From his posture and the way he held his arm, I was certain he was holding a pistol in his right hand and kept it aimed at the cashier. I observed years ago that a person holding a pistol with one hand will typically stand erect. When holding a weapon with both hands their shoulders will tend to lean forward which causes their upper body to slouch forward. I waited for the robber to move to a position where the gun would not be pointed at the cashier, and I would make my move. I could easily get the drop on him and gain an instant advantage. From the doorway, I could see most of the inside of the store. There was liquor displayed on shelves around the circumference of the room and two rows of shelving along the middle, creating three aisles. A counter with the cash register was to the right. What appeared to be premium liquors were displayed behind the checkout counter. Due to it being a recessed wall, there was an area of the room to my immediate left that I could not see. By the sound of a slight hum and vibration, I assumed beer and other refrigerated beverages were along that wall. After several seconds, the robber turned slightly to his left and while he and the cashier were looking out the front window of the store, he lowered the gun momentarily. I unholstered my service weapon as I sprang from my position and began giving the command for him to drop his weapon. My world went dark.

As my eyes opened, I realized I was lying in a pool of alcohol and broken glass on the floor of the store with my service weapon in my right hand. From what I observed, the only other person in the store was the cashier. The robber was not visible. I felt a strange cool sensation down the back of my neck. Moving to a kneeling position, with my left hand I reached around and felt the back of my neck. I could feel wetness. When I glanced at my hand it was covered in bright red blood.

The cashier approached me asking, "Sheriff, are you alright?"

"Yes. Was there more than one of them?"

"Yes, there were two. They just ran out the front of the store."

I rose to my feet, still unsure whether I had been shot or hit with a club of some kind. As I began moving toward the front door, the cashier grabbed me and asked, "Are you sure you are alright?"

I stopped for a few seconds, did a quick mental inventory, and replied, "Yes, I think I am okay."

I continued across the floor and out the front door as I saw two men in the small blue sedan pulling onto Main Street and traveling east. I was still close enough to see a small decal on the trunk lid. I could not quite read the decal, but it was reminiscent of the Hilltop Used Auto Sales decal on a vehicle owned by Jake Cummings. Jake had been the lead suspect in a homicide a couple of years earlier and ultimately died during an incident with county deputies.

I walked back into the store as Deputy Allen was arriving. As he entered the store his first instinct was to check my wound. I asked him whether it appeared I had been struck with some type of object. "It is difficult to tell, but it looks like you may have been shot. There is a small hole there, but the blood and your hair make it difficult to tell for sure," he commented with a concerned tone.

Deputy Allen radioed dispatch on his handheld and excitedly announced, "We need an ambulance at our location. Sheriff Rogers is wounded and needs to be checked out."

Deputy Allen turned toward the cashier and asked, "Was he shot or hit with something?"

"I think he was hit with a liquor bottle. I was facing away when the sheriff entered from the back room. I did not hear gunfire, so I assumed it was a liquor bottle. I heard a loud thud, bottles falling from the shelf, and the sheriff hitting the floor. Before running out of the store, the man with the gun stood over the sheriff for a few seconds pointing his gun at him. I thought he was going to shoot him."

"How long was I out?" I asked the cashier.

"Probably fifteen to twenty seconds, I guess. It happened so fast; I am not sure."

"Deputy Allen, I will take care of things here and get the cashier's statement. I need you to secure the area outside the building. Also, I need you to call Deputy Carter and ask her to go through our records and determine the final disposition of Jake Cummings' vehicle after he died. I think it was his car they were driving."

After interviewing the cashier, I determined the perpetrators got away with approximately two hundred dollars in cash and a couple of bottles of 'Sippers Whiskey,' a very rare and expensive whiskey not sold in many locations in this part of the country.

This type of crime is a rare event in our sleepy little town, but the fact that it appeared they were in Jake's car made it a real oddity. "Who would be driving that car?" I asked myself.

That was when I began to feel light-headed. I felt as though I might pass out and collapse to the floor again. I grabbed a folding chair from the storage room and sat for a minute. As I rose to my feet to continue working the scene, I realized I was not going to be on my feet for long. I returned to the chair. It was only a moment later a chorus of sirens arrived at the Package store.

Two paramedics were the first to enter the store. As soon as they saw the blood on my uniform shirt, they began checking my vital signs and examining the wound on the back of my head. "Sheriff, it looks like you have been shot. By the entry wound, it looks like a small caliber weapon. We need to get you to the hospital, clean this up, and get some X-rays to see if there is a bullet in there. How are you feeling?"

"I am light-headed and feel like a mule kicked me in the back of the head. Outside of that, I feel normal, I think. The cashier said he thought they clubbed me with a liquor bottle. I was not shot."

As I instructed Deputy Allen to work with city police and take statements from neighboring businesses, retrieve any available security video, and secure anything the perpetrators may have touched, the paramedics loaded me onto a gurney and rolled me into an ambulance. "Collect the neck of the broken liquor bottle for fingerprints. Maybe the guy who clubbed me was not wearing gloves," I commented.

As the Paramedic had commented earlier, I received a couple of X-rays along with a battery of other tests. Doctor John informed me that after they cleaned the wound it appeared I had been struck by an object that created a small 'V' shaped wound at the base of my skull.

He explained, "It would be consistent with being struck with a liquor bottle. If the bottle shattered when it contacted your head, it could easily leave that type of wound. We will clean it and stitch it up. Luckily, I did not see any skull fracture in the X-rays. It is not like the movies… you do not just break a liquor bottle over a person's head, and everybody keeps fighting. A liquor bottle is a serious weapon and can easily cause a skull fracture, even death. As long as you feel okay, we will let you go home, but concussion tests show that you have a serious concussion. So, we will keep you here for observation for a while. I will give you something for the pain and make you a little more comfortable. I know that must hurt and you are going to have some serious headaches for a few days."

"Yeah Doc, it hurts. If you would stop poking around on it, it might feel better. My head does hurt, but my biggest issue is that things are kind of cloudy right now. Things are foggy."

Doctor John replied, "That is from the concussion. You may feel that way for a day or two. As soon as I put some stitches in that wound, I will stop touching it and you can stop complaining."

As he shaved the area around my wound and stitched it, he commented, "Will, I was leaving for the day when the hospital and EMS received the call that you had been wounded. I knew I had to stay to treat you and make sure you were alright and received the best treatment we could provide. I have been your doctor since you were a little boy, and I wanted to make sure you were taken care of. While we are here, I will tell you, I never would have guessed you would become the sheriff of Carlin County."

I clarified, "Interim sheriff. This was my first day on the job. If it continues like this, I might not be interim sheriff for long. I guess most folks would agree that me in this role is a bit of a surprise. I would have never dreamed of it. But as you know Sheriff Joe was in a bad spot and asked for my help and I would do just about anything to help him. But in the end, it may have been him helping me, not me helping him. That is the way it has been with him for years, I was just slow to realize it."

"A man only learns in two ways, one by reading, and the other by association with smarter people."
– Will Rogers

Chapter Two

With the serious nature of my concussion, Doctor John insisted I spend a couple of days resting with no physical activity. It did not take long until I was overwhelmed with boredom and restlessness. My mind began to drift, and I reminisced back to Spring 2012 and how I became the interim sheriff of Carlin County.

It had been nearly two years since Jenni's murder and my life had settled back into a comfortable routine with James and Little Jenni. James was nine years old and Little Jenni was seven. We celebrated holidays, enjoyed some birthday parties, and attended numerous school activities. As expected, there had been some ups and downs for the kids, but the emotional issues were becoming less frequent. James and Little Jenni's adoption was crawling along at a painfully slow pace. Bruce had explained to me that due to Jenni being a homicide victim the case was unique, but he was confident and very reassuring about the eventual outcome. James and Little Jenni were becoming well-adjusted to life on the farm with me.

I had saddled my buckskin mare and spent the morning in the field working cattle. I had been keeping a watchful eye on a cow that was about to deliver a calf when lunch time rolled around. The kids had been playing along the creek bank and as was our routine, we all sat down for lunch together. As we were finishing lunch, I received a call from Sheriff Joe.

I answered the call with a welcoming, "It is great to hear from you Sheriff Joe. It has been a while."

"Yes, it has. We should not have these lapses in our visits. Will, are you and the kids going to be around the house this evening? I would like to stop by for a visit."

"School is out for spring break. So, we should all be here. I know your little deputies would love to see you. Is Betty coming with you? We have not seen her since the hayride."

"She asked me to apologize on her behalf, but she has something going on and will not be able to make it."

"What time do you want to come by? If you want, I will fire up the grill and cook some burgers or something. We have some fresh T-bone steaks I can put on."

"I appreciate the offer for supper, but that will not be necessary." I should be there around six o'clock."

"We will be looking for you around six then. I will ask James and Little Jenni to make us a fresh pitcher of tea. I know they will be excited that you are coming by for a visit."

As expected, Sheriff Joe pulled into the driveway a couple of minutes before six o'clock. James, Little Jenni, and I met him in the driveway. Sheriff Joe exited his car, knelt down, and greeted the kids with his customary handshake.

"Sheriff Joe it is good to see you. James and Little Jenni have been watching the road for two hours now waiting for you to get here. It is funny, after Jenni's murder, I always dreaded seeing your patrol car coming down the road, but now I find it to be a welcome sight. Take some time to visit with the kids. I have a cow about to drop a calf and need to run and check on her. Hopefully, I will be back in twenty minutes or so. If not, jump on a four-wheeler and follow the creek to the North two pastures up. I might need help pulling a calf."

As I returned to the house, I could see Sheriff Joe and the kids sitting on the porch. I parked my four-wheeler and walked over to them. Sheriff Joe commented, "I hope the cow and calf are alright. Do we need to go check on her?"

"It looks like they are going to be fine. She had the calf, and it was up moving around. Did you have a good visit with the kids?"

"You know that visiting with James and Little Jenni always puts a smile on my face. When you talk to them, it is easy to sense a warmth and sincerity about them. It is quite uncommon to talk to young kids that interact like that."

"They must have gotten that from their mom. She was always more social than me."

"Will, can we talk?" he asked.

"James, take Little Jenni and fix the sheriff and me a glass of iced tea please."

They returned with our tea, set the glasses down, and ran back into the house, Little Jenni chasing along behind James. Sheriff Joe and I took our seats where we had been on many previous occasions.

Sheriff Joe began, "Will, I have been county sheriff for nearly twenty years. I have known you for all that time and you know I am not a person who dances around issues, so I will get to the point. I have been diagnosed with a rare form of cancer. I would try to pronounce it for you but would only end up giving it a new name."

"Sheriff Joe, I don't know how to react to that."

"The doctors said there is not a lot of hope for treatment. They said chemo and radiation most likely would do nothing to prevent its spread. Even with treatment, they said the best I can hope for is a couple of years. Without treatment, they think maybe one year to a year and a half. I just do not see myself compromising what time I have left for treatment which will make the entire time miserable. I am assuming the lesser of the expectations and accepting that I may have one year. So, if I get anything past that, I will consider that a plus; a gift from above."

I commented, "I recently read an article about some new cancer treatments the University of Oklahoma is pioneering. Have you thought about that? If they think treatment won't help, have you considered going to the south part of the county to see a Medicine Man? I have always heard they can do some surprising things."

"Doctor John spoke to me about the new treatment at the University of Oklahoma. The Medicine Man is something I had not considered to this point. I know there is a guy who lives behind the store in Tall Tree that people say good things about. I may drive down there and see if I can visit with him about it."

"All I know to do is ask what I can do to help you. You know I will do anything I can. What do you need me to do?" I asked.

"There really is nothing you can do to impact the cancer or treatment, but there is something you can do for me personally. When I progress to the point where I can no longer perform my duties, I want you to finish my term as sheriff."

"Sheriff Joe, we both know my only experience with law enforcement has been on the other side of the role. I know nothing about being a law man."

Sheriff Joe replied, "When I ran for sheriff all those years ago, I had limited law enforcement experience. I had only served as a deputy for a short time. I have some time left and can teach you the things you need to know to get you a solid foundation. Will, I have known you for a long time. The reason I would like to see you take my office is that you are a good and honest man. When Jenni was murdered, the average person would have hidden and waited for me to uncover evidence and force me to come after them. You were honest enough to come forward. Even knowing that you would immediately become our lead person of interest in the case, you did not let fear steer you away from doing what you knew was right. Through all our conversations you were honest, straightforward, and as helpful as you could be. The county is at a time when we need to have an honest person in the Sheriff's office."

I laughed as I said, "Well it is about time we get an honest person in there."

Sheriff Joe laughed and then continued, "We need a person of your character. You can do good things for people in this role. You may not realize it, but I think that would give you some measure of satisfaction. Also, I need you to stop calling me Sheriff Joe. We are friends. We have shared times of pain, and we have shared times of joy. We have been through a lot together. You are a friend, Will, call me Joe."

I asked, "Even if I could do it, you cannot just appoint me can you?"

"I cannot, but the County Commissioners can. And they will listen to me when I plead the case to them. I do not expect an answer this minute, but obviously, time is limited for your response. At the end of the term, if you do not want to continue, you just do not run in the next election. You can go back to your farm life."

"Sheriff Joe, uh Joe, that is something beyond anything I would have ever considered. You know my life has always been on my farm."

"I need you to give it some thought and let me know," he replied. "If it is something you are willing to do, I will deputize you and start your training."

"That is something I would need to think about for a while."

"One last thing, Will, I have known about the cancer for a couple of weeks, but so far, outside of my family and Doctor John, nobody knows about my condition. I need it to stay that way until you make your decision."

"You might be right. I think I would receive some satisfaction from it if it allowed me to do good things for people. I have learned a few things during my time on this rock. One is that good men teach and do good things. Bad men teach and do bad things. My grandfather, a Cherokee elder, was not a person who spoke a lot. But you knew if he spoke, he was about to share words that had meaning. He taught me, "There are two paths in life. One is good, and one is bad. You will be confronted with the choice between the two paths every day of your life. If you have surrounded yourself with bad men, you will likely choose the path that leads to bad things. If you have surrounded yourself with good men, you will likely choose the path that leads to good things. You cannot walk both paths."

"Will, being the sheriff would give you an opportunity to teach and do good things for people. It will allow you to lead others along a path of good."

The Sheriff of Carlin County

He continued, "I do not think I have ever told you, but I knew your grandfather. He was a wise and respected man. When I met him, I was in my early twenties and had been drinking. I was driving along Walnut Ridge Road and had run my old truck off the road and was stuck in the ditch. No matter what I tried, I could not get out of the ditch. Your grandfather pulled alongside my old truck, looked at me, and asked whether I wanted some help. It did not take long before he apparently smelled the alcohol. As he latched a chain to my truck to pull it from the ditch, he asked, "Have you been drinking?"

"Yes sir."

"He asked, "Why?"

"I explained, "I guess I have been going through some stuff. I think my girlfriend has been messing around with another guy."

"He replied, "So you decided to get drunk? I will explain how I see things. If you have been drinking it is because you chose to drink. She had nothing to do with it. Only you chose to turn up a bottle. The decisions you make in your life are not dictated by things that happen around you. Your decisions come only from within you. It is good that you take responsibility for your decision though. As I got older and understood his message, it impacted me. I learned to be more judicious with my actions."

Sheriff Joe continued, "Will, like I said, take some time to decide whether this is something you want to pursue. If you choose to move forward, I will help you in any way I can to prepare you for service. If not, I understand. I am asking a lot from you."

"Sheriff Joe, I am flattered that you chose to approach me with this opportunity. But first, I need to get something off my chest. I lived for years thinking you and I were adversaries. Through those years with Jenni and Russell, I saw you as part of the problem. I saw you as a person who favored his family and refused to take action on Jenni's behalf. You told me that you had tried and did eventually successfully intervene. I thought I was fighting you all that time. I was wrong. Through all these years you have been nothing but kind and helpful to me. Maybe a bit harsh through my drunken days, but always a friend. I was not. Through the entire ordeal with Jenni's murder, you were understanding and helpful. Thank you for that. Like a respected friend said to me one time… that is the end of that discussion."

"Thank you, Will. I have one final request. As things progress with the cancer, I would like to spend some time here. Behind the barn, where you had the wienie roast, is the prettiest and most tranquil place I have seen on this earth. As I make my final peace with our creator, it would be the perfect place to be alone with my thoughts. I realize it may be an odd request, but it would mean a lot to me."

"I will tell James and Little Jenni if they see you back there to give you space. I will explain that there will be times when you just do not feel like visiting. Spend as much time here as you would like. Treat the place as your own."

"The worst thing that happens to you may be the best thing for you if you don't let it get the best of you."
  – Will Rogers

Chapter Three

Life on the farm for James and Little Jenni was somewhat carefree, but they had chores they were responsible for each day. They were not difficult things to do, but they were responsibilities. They were paid a weekly wage for completing their chores. During the summer months they had opportunities to earn additional money by picking and selling blackberries, which grew plentifully in untended areas of the farm. Like when I was a child, they earned a good sum selling them. I thought today would be a good opportunity to let James and Little Jenni enjoy the fruits of their labor.

I explained, "A fun part of earning money is occasionally getting to spend it for things you want, but do not necessarily need. It has been a few days since Sheriff Joe came to the house and I need to go into town to meet with him again. I will drop you off at Mr. Henderson's store and let you shop. You may take twenty dollars of your money and spend it on anything your heart desires."

I walked the kids into Henderson's store and visited with Mr. Henderson. I explained that I have a brief meeting and would be leaving the kids there. He promised to keep an eye on them. He turned to James and Little Jenni and commented, "If you are looking for toys, you will find them in the basement."

I paused for a moment to reflect on the old store. I had many memories of walking the well-worn wooden floor, up and down the aisles looking for hidden treasures. The aged homemade wooden shelves were packed with inventory; some old and some new. Much of the inventory remained from probably the 1960's and 1970's. If you were looking for old hardware items, this was the place to shop. Mr. Henderson still believed in stocking things made to withstand use and the effects of time, not the cheaper disposable items constructed of plastic. I was happy that Mr. Henderson had managed to withstand the competition of the chain retail stores and their deep pockets. I guess there were enough folks like me that were willing to pay a couple of dollars more for an item to help him continue his livelihood. Many old family-owned stores like this have not survived the competition and are becoming hard to find.

I told the kids, "Take your time. I will pick you up in half an hour or so."

As previously arranged, Sheriff Joe and I met at his office. Following our greetings and handshake, I explained, "After my divorce from Laura Smith, I was sober and learned to find comfort in routine. That is when the things I do in my life were cast to a steady, consistent beat like a metronome. I am solid as long as I do not venture too far from that routine and get out of rhythm. I think that had been my way of staying sober. When I took in James and Little Jenni, my routine was shattered. But I have been able, with some success, to establish some routine things in my life with them. They are not a burden to care for, and they seem to be agreeable with my daily routines. I think it helps them feel some sense of security."

"I understand that, Will."

"I must admit, those old demons have tried to creep back into my life. They invite me into every bar and liquor store I pass. But having James and Little Jenni has given me a purpose and has helped me fend off those demons. Sometimes I swear they can sense me getting edgy and know I need help. Being the sheriff, running two farms, and raising two small children would pretty much make having any sort of routine impossible. Honestly, I have concerns with bringing that much chaos into my life."

"But like I said, being sheriff will allow you an opportunity to have a positive impact on people. Maybe that purpose, along with raising James and Little Jenni, will carry you through. But opportunity is all I have to offer." he replied.

I replied, "I think having a positive impact on people would be rewarding and is the only reason I would even consider your request. With that said, I want to see if I can make it work."

"Will, I am excited and thankful that you will give it a try. If I did not believe that it is something you will enjoy and do well, I would have never mentioned it to you."

"Joe, I have no idea how to make it work financially. I cannot work two farms and have a full-time job. I do not have anybody to be with James and Little Jenni when I am not able to be home. Income from the farms is not enough to hire someone full-time to manage cattle and crops and maintain fences, barns, and equipment. I assume a sheriff's salary is not enough to allow me to have a virtually full-time babysitter. I can lease Jenni's place and earn a little. But I will have to continue to run my farm."

"Like I said before, my health condition demands we start your training soon. If we start next Monday, that will give you a week to find someone to watch the kids. The rest, we will have to figure out as we go."

"As I said, I want to do this for the opportunity to help people. To follow up on your story about meeting my grandfather when you were younger, there is more to understanding his words. He told you that only you are responsible for your decisions; that is true for all of us. I do not make decisions for you. You do not make decisions for me. Therefore, the way that I impact your decisions in a positive way is to be an example of what is good and right. That means that I affect your decisions by how I live my life. This job will hopefully provide visibility and will allow me the opportunity to impact folks' lives.

"Yes it will," he replied.

I was at Joe's office early on Monday morning. He wasted no time beginning my training.

He began, "We have a tremendous number of things to cover. Let's get started. Something you need to understand, nothing will prepare you for your initial interactions with a criminal, especially violent cases. You may have seen a thousand times on television when an officer engages or interacts with a criminal. You may think that gives you an idea of what it will be like. It does not. Those images are from the perspective of a viewer. As a law enforcement officer, you are not a viewer, you are a participant. When you see the pure evil behind violent criminals and their actions, you are seeing and experiencing it in real life. It is a different perspective. It is like seeing from within your soul because you are totally invested at that moment. It becomes almost surreal. Hopefully, you and I can get through enough of those events to get you accustomed to that feeling and how to control the rush of adrenaline you will experience."

Riding with Sheriff Joe for the next several months, we had opportunities for me to gain exposure to various criminal activities. One incident was particularly impactful for me. Late one Thursday afternoon, we received a call from a local bar. They had reported that their bartender had been shot during a quarrel with his ex-wife. I realized this was going to be a valuable opportunity for me to watch Joe and see how he interacted with people during the investigation of a serious crime.

We arrived at the bar, and I was surprised to see the bartender gathering his personal effects from behind the counter. Sheriff Joe asked the man to have a seat at a table located at the end of the bar near the door. As we waited for an ambulance, Sheriff Joe questioned the bartender to learn the details of the incident. As I sat down at the table beside the bartender, it was easy to see a small hole in the center of his forehead about one-half inch higher than his eyebrows. Occasionally I looked away from the bartender and tried to take in the sights around the bar. Although it was a small property with probably no more than a dozen or so tables, the room was dark except for the lighting provided directly behind the bar, and one lone light hanging above a pool table in the back right corner. Adjacent to the pool table was a small dance floor and a makeshift stage for live music. One sliver of light shone through a window where a red velveteen curtain did not cover the full span of the window. It caused a mild discomfort in me that it was difficult to see the faces of bar patrons. I found it odd that none of the patrons appeared to be concerned or upset that the Bartender had been shot. Making things worse for me was the demon in my head repeatedly telling me to call out to the Bar Maid for a drink. I asked myself, "Will the desire for a drink never leave me?"

Sheriff Joe asked the man, "How long did you wait before they called? There is a significant amount of blood down your face and neck and on your shirt. It has obviously been a while since you were shot, all the blood is dry."

The bartender explained, "I went outside to talk to my ex-wife. She became irate when I would not agree to come home with her after work. She pulled a small .22 caliber revolver from her purse and shot me."

"Didn't it hurt?" Sheriff Joe asked.

"Yeah, it stung pretty good, and it burned. If you have never been shot, you would not believe how much it burned," he replied.

"But you continued talking with her after she shot you?" Without a response previously, Joe reworded and repeated his first question. "How much longer did you talk?" Joe asked.

He replied, "Probably 45 minutes or so, I guess. That woman is crazy. She would not listen to me. I could not reason with her."

As we heard the sirens of an ambulance approaching, he commented, "I am not going to the hospital."

Joe placed his hand on the guy's shoulder and tried to reason with him. "Sir, you need to go to the hospital and get checked out. Presumably, you have a bullet in your head and need to have x-rays to check."

"Am I in any trouble with the law?" he asked. "Am I under arrest?"

Joe replied, "No sir. It does not appear you have violated any laws, but I strongly encourage you to go to the hospital and get checked out."

He rose from his seat, grabbed his keys from behind the bar, and commented, "If I am not in trouble with the law, I am going home."

As we walked out of the bar and into a small gravel parking lot, the Bartender continued, "I am not sure if it matters, but I will not press charges against her if that is required. She may be my ex, but I do not want to see her get into any trouble."

Joe replied, "Actually, she has committed a couple of crimes. We do not need you to press charges."

The bartender replied, "If you press charges on her, I will testify that it was an accident. I do not want her to get into trouble."

We watched as he walked past the paramedics, got into his pickup truck, and drove away.

We returned a few days later to follow up with the bartender to determine whether he'd had a change of heart regarding charges being filed against his ex-wife. As disturbing as it had been seeing him covered in dried blood days earlier, his later appearance was even more disturbing. You could clearly see the hole in his forehead. His skin from the gunshot wound to his chin was an odd grayish-blue color. I struggled to maintain eye contact with him.

After several minutes of discussion, he advised, "I will not support charges being filed against her." Sheriff Joe never sought charges against the ex-wife.

During my training period, we had the opportunity to see numerous incidents and situations. We had some laughs and good times as well. Through my time riding and training with Sheriff Joe, I often had a good laugh at him and his frustration with his patrol car. On occasion when Sheriff Joe needed to accelerate in pursuit of another vehicle, as the speedometer hit forty-five mph, the engine of his patrol car would spit and sputter until he reached fifty-five mph. It would then accelerate as expected. He commented that they had been trying to identify and fix the issue for more than a year but had been unsuccessful. He would lay down a few choice profanities and keep his foot on the pedal as he waited for it to run properly.

During patrols one afternoon, I asked, "Joe, did you ever get into a tussle with anyone?"

"Will, if you do this job, you are going to have physical confrontations. Yes, I've had to scatter gravel with fellows more than a couple of times during my tenure. I am okay wrestling a man if he needs it, but I have always had a difficult time with females. I am an old-fashioned guy and was raised to never lift my hand to a woman. You must limit the physical interaction with them. If you have to wrestle them, get them cuffed as quickly as you can. Do not allow the confrontation to continue."

"Get someone else to blow your horn and the sound will carry twice as far."
— **Will Rogers**

Chapter Four

As instructed a couple of days prior, Deputy Carter had been checking records to determine the final disposition of Jake Cummings' vehicle. "Sheriff, first, I must tell you our records were a mess. That is something we need to clean up. That took much longer than it should have. Second, the person who picked up Jake's car was a guy named James King. The paperwork says he is the son of Jake Cummings. His residence is listed as Tremont, Missouri. We followed up with Missouri DMV and learned that the vehicle is now registered to a man named Rodney Rickert."

It only took a minute for me to look up Tremont, Missouri on my phone. It is a small town in Twain County, not far from Salem, Missouri.

I yelled to the outer office, "Beverly, get the Sheriff of Twain County, Missouri on the phone.

Tell them we need information on a resident up there."

Only a couple of minutes later, Beverly transferred the call to my office and advised, "The sheriff of Twain County is Sheriff Matthews."

Deputy Carter and I introduced ourselves and explained our situation. It took several minutes but after discussions with Sheriff Matthews, we verified that James King is the son of Jake Cummings. It turned out that between stints in prison, Jake had a child with a woman he had lived with for a while. Apparently, their son took her family's name. The Sheriff's office had numerous incidents involving James King. The sheriff commented that he and his deputies know James and the family well.

Sheriff Matthews asked, "Did anybody get a tag number from the car at the robbery?"

I replied, "No, apparently they removed the tag before driving to the liquor store."

I added, "I had some ugly history with Jake Cummings. I suspect they may have wanted to do me harm."

He replied, "Sheriff Rogers, James, and his kin are some violent characters. If they were involved in this, watch yourself. They will probably be back. We suspect them of some serious violent assaults here, but we can never collect enough evidence to file charges. Folks around here will not provide statements against them."

I responded, "Trust me, we will be watching for them. I am all but certain that was Jake Cummings' car."

Sheriff Matthews continued, "I can tell you James King is closest to his half-brother, Rodney Rickert. They are dangerous. When they are together, they each feed off the other's violent nature. If there were two people involved in the liquor store robbery and either of them was involved, I can almost assure you they were both involved. You are most likely looking for both of them. If it was them, they have probably returned to Tremont."

"Could you let us know if they are up there?" I asked.

Sheriff Matthews replied, "We will check and let you know. Also, we will ask around to see if we can determine if they made any out-of-town trips recently."

"Sheriff Matthews, could you send us the names of the family members most likely to visit our area with bad intentions? Descriptions and tag numbers of their vehicles would be helpful as well. Thank you for your time and your assistance. We will be in touch soon."

Following our conversation with Sheriff Matthews, I informed Deputy Carter that I wanted her to head up the investigation into the liquor store robbery.

She expressed her excitement that I entrusted her to lead an important investigation. She told me, "One thing I noticed when driving by the store is that the cashier's vehicle has a Missouri license plate. Do you want me to run the plate?" She asked.

"Yeah, run the plate, and let's see where he is from. I knew I did not know the man but had not given much thought to it."

I offered some thoughts on the investigation, "Go back to the liquor store and interview the cashier again. If you get anything alarming back on the license plate, question him a few times and observe his reaction to being questioned. Also, I have such a strong gut feeling about James King and his half-brother being involved, ask Sheriff Matthews if they can start applying a little psychological pressure up there. An occasional drive by James King's house just to let them know they are in our sights. Run a criminal background check on the cashier. One last thing, interview the owner of the liquor store. See what they can tell you about the cashier."

"I will run the plate on the car and follow up with Sheriff Matthews."

"Nothing obvious… just cruise by James King's house while on patrol. Oh, something that keeps nagging at me, when I started to chase the suspects at the liquor store, the cashier stopped me to ask if I was alright. He held onto my arm and blocked my way to the door. It didn't seem like a big thing at the time, but I just cannot shake the feeling that he was buying them a few extra seconds to get away."

When we received the names, vehicle descriptions, and tag numbers from Sheriff Matthews, I instructed Deputy Carter to place the information in every county patrol car, share it with local police departments, and cover all details at each shift meeting for a few days.

For a while, I could feel my pulse quicken each time I saw a vehicle with Missouri license plates. Even though we had been given information about specific vehicles to watch for, it still immediately piqued my attention.

Two days later, I called Sheriff Matthews to follow up and see what he had learned and could share. Maybe he would have some details we needed to move forward with our investigation.

"Sheriff Rogers, I was getting ready to give you a call. I have verified that James and his brother are in Tremont but were out of town for a couple of days recently."

"If you have an opportunity to check their vehicle, it would be good to know if they have a bottle or two of Sippers Whiskey with them. Also, we have a security video from a nearby business. There is a video of two men exiting the car and putting on ski masks as they enter the store. The quality is not good, but if we send it, will you and your deputies see if you recognize the two men?"

"Send the video now and we will look at it. Rest assured, if we have an opportunity to pull them over, we will look for the Sippers Whiskey bottles," he replied.

"Thanks. The robbers managed to get away with a couple of hundred dollars and a couple of bottles of this whiskey. It is pretty rare around here and might serve as evidence of who was involved," I replied.

During our shift meeting the following morning, Deputy Carter provided an update on the investigation.

She explained, "After some follow up we learned the cashier had only been working at the store for a couple weeks. One detail that stands out is the store security camera became disabled two days prior to the robbery. Sheriff Matthews notified us that the quality of the video from the neighboring business was too poor, and they were not able to make a positive identification of the suspects. Fortunately, we realized there may be additional video available. I remembered that the car wash was having vandalism issues last year and installed a couple of security cameras. So, I thought I would pay Johnny Marchand a visit and see if they inadvertently caught anything on camera. Johnny knew about the robbery and you getting clubbed over the head. He felt bad that he had not even thought about his cameras."

I interrupted and asked, "Did you have any luck with that?"

"Thankfully, he only deletes old videos every few months. His camera has a different angle and has footage of a couple of locals coming out of the liquor store just before the robbers donned their ski masks and went into the store. It was the Johnson twins, Ricky and Robbie. I have a meeting with them this afternoon after they get off work. Hopefully, they will have some information or descriptions of the suspects. The cashier's vehicle license plate came back as a St. James, Missouri address. St. James is about a twenty-minute drive from Tremont. One last thing – the guy who clubbed you over the head must have been wearing gloves as well. There were no fingerprints on the bottle neck."

"Have you checked Charlie's Burger Barn for video and witnesses?" I asked.

Carter replied, "We did, but it was a dead end."

"That is tremendous progress. It looks like you are covering the bases. Keep Deputy Kingfisher involved as you continue. I hope you are working with the city police department as well," I commented.

She replied, "I have extended invitations for city detectives to be involved but they commented they have so much on their plates, that they do not have the manpower. They requested that if we learn anything they should know, to give them a heads-up."

"If the car wash video is better quality than we had before, send it to Sheriff Matthews. Maybe they can make an ID from this video. Does the video have a good date and time stamp?"

"Will do. Yes, the date and time match the records from the county Dispatcher. I will let you know what I get from the Johnson twins. I will take James King and Rodney Rickert's pictures with me when I meet with them," Carter replied.

Nearly one week passed before the next update on the investigation. During that week, deputies Carter and Kingfisher made tremendous progress.

Deputy Carter described their interview with the cashier. "We have gone back and interviewed the cashier again. I am not sure whether it was just me, or if the cashier started getting nervous. He was not able to maintain eye contact at all."

Kingfisher commented, "I thought he was clearly nervous."

Deputy Carter continued, "We will stop by again in a couple of days."

"This time when you interview him, one of you asks the questions while the other takes notes. Maintain eye contact with him and write with some enthusiasm."

"If you interview him again and he gets visibly nervous, he will probably rabbit on us. He will likely head back to St. James."

Kingfisher interjected, "Sheriff Matthews reported they are making routine patrols past James King's residence and a couple of other family members' homes. He and his deputies were able to make a positive identification of James King from the car wash security video, but there was no footage providing an opportunity to identify the other suspect. From the time he exited the vehicle, his back was to the camera."

Carter continued, "We interviewed the liquor store owner. He said he knew very little about the cashier. He likes the guy and commented that he is a good worker. One thing he noted was there were no missing bottles of Sippers Whiskey. What is supposed to be in inventory is accounted for. Since he takes inventory every weekend, he is confident in his inventory numbers."

"Why would the cashier tell us they took bottles of a particular brand of whiskey?" I asked.

Kingfisher replied, "It makes no sense to us. We cannot think of a reason why. Unless he intended to take a couple of bottles for himself and then decided against it later."

"We ran the criminal background on the cashier, and it came back clean. One lone traffic ticket was all there was," Carter added.

"Wow. I knew you two would do a great job, but you have moved this thing forward this much in a matter of a couple of weeks. Do you think the cashier was in on it?"

"Yes sir, we do. If it was James King, it would be the perfect setup to get you in the store if they wanted to do you harm," Carter replied. "That might be a motive beyond a simple robbery," she added.

"Then continue putting pressure on the cashier and let's see how he responds. St. James may not be in his county but ask Sheriff Matthews if he knows the cashier. If he does, and if he associates with the King family, it is time to turn up the heat on James King and his brother. If you think he was involved, ask the D.A. if we can pursue a conspiracy charge on the cashier."

She added, "We conducted our interview with Ricky and Robbie Johnson. They were very helpful. We could see from the video that as they passed on the sidewalk in front of the store, one of the robbers lightly brushed Ricky. Ricky turned and looked at the guy as they went on their way. Ricky said he remembered the guy fairly well. Looking at the picture, he thought it might be the half-brother, Rodney Rickert, but he could not say with certainty that it was. They were both confident that the other one was James King. We will get more pictures of the family in front of them as soon as we can."

It was a few days later when Carter and Kingfisher conducted our final update meeting for the liquor store robbery. I kicked off our meeting by asking, "Are we ready to issue an arrest warrant for James King?"

Kingfisher replied, "Yes sir. We believe we are for James King, but without identification from the Johnson twins or the video, we do not have enough for a warrant on Rickert. Unless we can get King to roll over on him, we have nothing."

"Review where you are with the D.A. and see if they agree we can issue a warrant. Guys, I have only been here a matter of weeks and want to make sure we do everything we have to do to ensure we do not lose King on a technicality. The D.A. will work with Twain County and file. Let's get King in here and keep working on getting his half-brother if he was the second suspect. He would be the one who tried to crack my skull with a liquor bottle."

A warrant was requested for James King and issued. Sheriff Matthews and his deputies served the warrant and made the arrest with limited physical resistance.

The Sheriff of Carlin County

It took several days of judicial process, but James King was released to our custody. Deputy Carter and I drove to Twain County, picked him up, and transported him back to the Carlin County jail.

While being questioned, he told me, "Sheriff, my dad has a lot of family in the hills back home and they are going to keep coming after you until we get satisfaction for what you did to him. You will never know when or where, but we will always be there waiting for our chance to get our revenge."

"This may not be the old Wild West, but I can assure you, if any of your family comes looking for me, they will be arrested and sent to jail, or I will send them back to Missouri in a box. Any way it goes from here, it will not be you. At least not for several years. You will be sitting in an Oklahoma prison. I will see to that. You need to always remember, you may think you can get the jump on me, but you will always wonder if I have set the stage for you like I did for your daddy."

"We already got the jump on you once. I just didn't finish it. That was my mistake. If those guys had not seen us going into the liquor store, I would have finished it," he replied angrily.

"Do you realize that you are not a very good criminal? You were seen on two security cameras, and we have two eyewitnesses. We would not have had a better video if it was a Hollywood movie. My deputies solved this case in short order. You are going to be sitting in an Oklahoma prison by yourself. Your family is letting you take the blame for the robbery, and the assault of a peace officer. Your brother, Rodney, and the cashier will be walking around free men while you sit in a cell for the next several years. I admit that you got the jump on me, but at that time I did not know we were playing. Now I do."

"We can't all be heroes, because somebody has to sit on the curb and clap as they go by."
– Will Rogers

Chapter Five

James and Little Jenni's adoption took longer to complete than even our attorney Bruce would have imagined, but as he had continually reassured us of the eventual outcome, it was final on Thursday, June thirteenth, 2013. For a celebration, the church hosted a small adoption party for us following Sunday services a few days later. After the party, Shelley Corntassel commented, "Will, now that the adoption is final, I have something I have wanted to discuss with you for a while. I want you, James, and Little Jenni to come to my house for dinner. It would be a good chance for you to relax for a while and let the kids play together."

"That sounds like a good time. When would you like to do that?"

"Saturday evening around five o'clock would be good. That will give me some time to prepare something special for you and the kids. What is your favorite meal?"

"My favorite meal? Hmm. Let me see. I would have to say good southern fried chicken with homemade mashed potatoes."

As she walked away, she turned, and with a big smile said, "We will see you, James, and Little Jenni on Saturday."

That Saturday afternoon I instructed James and Little Jenni to put on some nice clothes and we left for Shelley's house.

As promised, Shelley had prepared my favorite dinner. As we sat, her girls entertained us with details about school and friends, and their plans and hopes for the summer and upcoming school year. We often think that times are different for our children than they were for us, but they still deal with the same issues we did. The difference seems to be that the consequences are more extreme for them. We lived in a carefree world where we could ride our bikes or walk down the street alone. These modern times require them to be more aware and vigilant than we ever needed to be.

After dinner, while the kids were playing games in one of Shelley's daughter's rooms, Shelley and I sat at the table and talked. She reached across the table, placed her hand over mine, and said, "Will, you obviously are a good and honest man. You are an intelligent man. But I apparently am too subtle with my flirtation. I have never been quite so direct with anybody, but I would like to go on a date with you."

I sat for a few seconds in silence. I was stunned by her proposal and surprised that I had not recognized any advances from her over the past couple of years. I smiled as I told her, "I thought there was a Mr. Corntassel. I have been wondering all evening where he is. I have been waiting for him to come walking in."

She laughed as she replied, "There has not been a Mr. Corntassel for several years now. I wanted to talk to you when I arrived at your farm for the hayride but realized it could create issues with you being involved in an ongoing custody case, especially this case."

"This entire time I have been calling you Mrs. Corntassel with James and Little Jenni. I thought you were married."

She continued, "When you were a senior in high school, I had a major crush on you. I may have only been a seventh grader, but I often saw you at ball games and school events. I realized then you were too old to date me, or I might have told you then."

"It's funny, I thought that on the evening of the hayride, there was something you wanted to say but did not. I would have never dreamed that was it. I assumed it was something related to the children."

"I also want to offer you some help. I know the new job as sheriff and running two farms leaves you limited social time, and it cannot be easy trying to arrange around-the-clock care for James and Little Jenni. Whether we date or not, I want to help you with the kids. Mary, my oldest, is old enough and responsible enough to help with the kids. While school is out for the summer, you can drop them off in the morning and Mary can watch them until I get home in the afternoon. We will take care of them in the evening until you pick them up. If a situation arises and you need to work into the night, they can stay with us as long as they need. When school starts in late August, James and Little Jenni would ride the school bus to my house after school."

I clarified, "Interim sheriff. I know I would enjoy spending time with you and that is an attractive arrangement, but that would be a burden on you and the girls. I cannot ask you to do that."

"You are not asking, I am offering. I am a parent and the Administrator of Child Protective Services. I understand what caring for those kids requires." she replied.

"Admittedly, I am struggling with babysitters, and it has only been a few weeks now. I do have a sitter lined up for the next week or so though. I will pay Mary for taking care of the kids.

Smiling, she replied, "I am sure we can agree on a little something for Mary."

"Are you and the girls busy next Friday night? We can try this out and see how it goes. You and I can go to dinner and the kids can stay with the girls. I would enjoy taking you to dinner and we can see how things go with the kids."

"I know we have nothing going on Friday. It is a date."

We both laughed as I told her, "I have never dated a married woman before."

A date is something I have not done for several years and I found myself nervous as I dressed for dinner with Shelley. James and Little Jenni were excited to see Shelley and her daughters, Mary and Madison. They got to know Shelley well while they were in CPS custody for those months, and they developed a sense of trust with her. We arrived at Shelley's and spent a while talking and letting the kids get settled before Shelley and I left for dinner. Following Shelley's instructions to call if the girls needed anything, we were on our way to dinner.

Aware that I am not a particularly social person, I was concerned that conversation might get slow during dinner, but we did not struggle to find topics to discuss.

"Shelley, I never could have dreamed the number of children's cases you deal with. Even in a rural county, you have a surprising number of cases. I had no idea the amount of time you spend with the Sheriff's office. It is sad that is necessary. Now that I know you are not married, I must say I do enjoy seeing you on a routine basis. Your smile is a pleasant and welcome thing during the long days in the office. It always brightens my day."

Sheriff Joe was a topic of much of our conversation. I explained, "I have noted that Joe is a guy who is always in charge of every situation he is involved in. He is not a follower. He is one-hundred percent leader. When he speaks, people tend to listen. He is a powerful personality, but still shows compassion for folks when it is needed."

She replied, "Yes, he is definitely in charge wherever he goes, and I often see his kind and gentle side when dealing with our cases. He does a great job with the kids."

"It takes a special and rare person to have that level of confidence and strength. I do not know whether I will ever be able to become that guy. And I believe that having that in-command attitude is necessary to be a strong leader in law enforcement. It certainly gives me something to work to achieve."

"You may not believe you have that character, but many people watched you through the entire investigation of Jenni's homicide and how you handled James and Little Jenni. And how you have managed two farms while adopting two small children. We all noticed. You may have more strength and confidence than you give yourself credit for. I think that is the reason my childhood crush was re-kindled."

"I am not sure I know how to respond to that. That is a tall compliment and I have never handled compliments well. To me, stepping up for the kids is just what any person would do."

"My older brother, Sammy, always told me you were different than the other guys in school. He always spoke highly of you and how you carried yourself… with confidence. He said that even when you were young you were comfortable and confident in every situation. It seems to me that you may already be part of the way to becoming that leader."

She continued, "When I told Sammy you were adopting the children, he was not surprised. He said that is just what you would do. Will, not everybody would turn their life upside down and adopt two small children. James being your son may make things a little different but adopting both children took an uncommon level of selflessness and compassion. It took a serious level of sacrifice."

"Okay, you can stop now. I want to hear more about the crush you had on me," I said as we laughed.

I continued, "As I discussed with Sheriff Joe, I took this job for the opportunity to have a positive impact on people's lives. I am a simple farmer and carpenter, but I think I have things to offer that can help folks."

"I am sure of that," she replied.

"I have one serious concern though. If you spend time with me there may be personal repercussions for you and the girls. There will be folks who will not like me. And being associated with me will have consequences," I said.

"I already have that issue in my life. Trust me, when you remove children from a home, their parents are not going to like you. I can accept the bitterness of narrow-minded people, Will."

"I had not thought of what you already endure, but I needed to put my concern out there."

We finished dinner and returned to Shelley's house. James and Little Jenni ran to the door to meet us and immediately asked, "May we spend the night here?"

"I think we have asked enough from Mary and Madison for one night. Thank them and let's go home. Maybe we will come back another night," I told them as I peered over at Shelley.

While giving James and Little Jenni a hug, Shelley smiled and told them, "You will be back many times."

As the kids ran out the door, Shelley walked me to the door, looked me in the eyes, and said, "Let's not make this uncomfortable." She placed her right hand on my shoulder, leaned toward me, and kissed me.

"That certainly answered that question for me," I commented.

"We are adults and do not need to pretend we did not both want to know what that would be like. That was nice," she said.

I managed to muster a reply, "It was." I began to walk away, but turned and kissed her, a bit deeper and a bit longer. "Yeah, that was nice," I said with a smile, turned, and walked to the car.

As we drove home, James and Little Jenni chattered constantly about the things they had done that evening. It was comforting to learn that they had enjoyed their time with Mary and Madison. My mind was preoccupied with my evening as well. Especially the kiss at the door.

I did remember Shelley from when she was in junior high. She was a pretty girl, but as she had said, too young at that time. Admittedly, I still found her to be very attractive, but as I had explained to her, I thought she was married. Thinking that, I obviously had never given any thought to dating her. Learning that she was not married, I was now receptive to the idea.

"Good judgment comes from experience, and a lot of that comes from bad judgment."
– **Will Rogers**

Chapter Six

Leaders in any organization probably have favored employees or members. Whether that is advisable or not, it is inevitable. I am sure having favored employees goes against some management textbook somewhere, but there will always be those individuals who perform above the rest. As the interim sheriff, I dealt with many of the same issues as most businesses. Such things as pay, morale, performance, attendance, and employee development are an integral part and critical to leading the department. Like in business, a leader in law enforcement should value every person evenly and strive to develop them in a similar manner. Let me tell you I tried, but I had two deputies who day in, and day out stood above the rest. Of course, being in a rural county, I only had nine full-time deputies, but deputies Allen and Carter were high performers and the ones I could turn to for any situation that arose. I had asked Joe early in my training process who his best deputies were. Typical Joe, when I asked, he told me he would not bias my opinion and answer that question. But it did not take long for me to see the difference between them and the rest of my deputies.

Being a rural county with a limited number of deputies, and having a large county to cover, our deputies are typically required to patrol solo. But I initiated a practice where each deputy rides with me for one-half of a shift, once per month. It gave me an opportunity to hear what each deputy sees in the field. And it was a great time to get to know them personally and the issues they were facing outside of work. And of course, they all offered learning opportunities for me.

It had been an active day in the county and Deputy Allen was doing his ride-along with me. We were dispatched to a remote part of the county for a domestic violence call. From the beginning of my time as interim sheriff, I found most domestic violence issues to be especially egregious and disturbing. I was anxious to respond to the call. As we left the last paved road and transitioned onto a gravel road, a Ford pickup fell in behind us. I had been watching the pickup in my rearview mirror for a mile or so when they accelerated and began closing in on us. Not knowing whether this might be a person related to the call we were on, I slowed my patrol car and moved to the edge of the road. Although this part of the county is generally heavily timbered, we were entering a long section of roadway passing through an open clearing. This gave me a wide shoulder on the road allowing them to pull alongside us. That would give them an opportunity to let us know if they were in distress. As I continued to slow my patrol car, I thought I heard a shot from a small caliber weapon. I looked at Deputy Allen and asked if he heard anything.

"Yes, sheriff, that sounded like a gunshot."

That is when the truck accelerated and began to drive past us. As they neared my patrol car, a hail of gunshots rang out. I could hear numerous bullets hitting my patrol car as the Ford pickup continued accelerating past us. I accelerated and began pursuit. As my patrol car hit 45 mph it began to spit and sputter. I yelled some of Joe's previous profanities as I continued pumping the gas pedal trying to keep pace with the Ford pickup. Eventually, we began to accelerate again. Luckily the Ford pickup was still in sight. I yelled to the deputy, "Allen, when I catch them, I need you to return fire." He did not respond, so I repeated, "Allen, I will need you to return fire."

While trying to keep my patrol car on the gravel road, I looked over at Deputy Allen. He was leaning against the door and was not responding. I slid to a stop on the shoulder of the road as Deputy Allen struggled to say, "I am hit." I could see a small stream of blood running from his hairline and down his neck behind his ear. I yelled, "Allen, talk to me."

Immediately I grabbed the radio and told dispatch, "Shots fired. I have a deputy down. I need an ambulance and available units on Farm Road 117. We are 2 miles south of Old Peter's Prairie Road. Hurry! Suspects were last seen heading south on Farm Road 117 in a two-tone brown 1996 Ford Club cab pickup."

The Dispatcher replied, "Shots fired on Farm Road 117. Deputy down. Is that correct?"

I replied, "Yes. I need an ambulance now. Allen is down. Send life-flight if they are available."

"Keep talking to me, deputy." He only let out a slow soft moan and then became silent.

I jumped from my patrol car and pulled Allen from the passenger side. As I laid his head and back against the side of the patrol car, I continued calling his name. I checked his pulse. Nothing. As I laid him in the grass, I looked at his face as I told him, "I've called for backup and an ambulance. Talk to me Allen," I repeated.

I rolled him onto his back. His eyes were open, but it was easy to see there was no life behind them. I hit the emergency number on my phone and laid it on the ground beside him.

As I was beginning chest compressions the Dispatcher answered. "Patch me through to secure comms and link in the ambulance and all county units," I yelled.

"Talk to me, Allen. Stay with me."

As I maintained a watchful eye for the Ford pickup to double back and take another pass at us, I performed chest compressions and continued speaking to dispatch. "I need one county unit here and one unit en route on Highway 57 to where Farm Road 117 intersects with it north of the Harrelson place. Again, it is a two-tone brown 1996 Ford Club cab pickup. No license plate. I would assume when they get to Highway 57, they will turn and go northbound and away from town. I want them caught."

The Dispatcher's message was prompt and directed county Unit 2, Deputy Carter, to respond to my location and Unit 4, Deputy Andrews, to respond to the north on Highway 57.

I continued chest compressions until life-flight and medical support arrived and they relieved me. It was only a few minutes later they placed an automated CPR device on Deputy Allen and onto a stretcher. He was loaded into the helicopter and was en route to the hospital. Considering the seriousness of his wound, they chose to fly him directly to a trauma hospital in Tulsa.

As soon as she arrived, I directed Deputy Carter to secure the scene and I jumped in my patrol car and joined the search for the Ford truck. I continued down Farm Road 117 searching for any sign of the truck. I checked every side road and farmhouse along the way. But eventually, I intersected Highway 57. Knowing that Deputy Andrews had gone northbound, I decided to turn south in case the suspects had doubled back toward town. We searched for more than an hour but saw no signs of the truck. I instructed Deputy Andrews to return to the scene and begin collecting and marking evidence.

I returned to the scene and provided a detailed statement and walked Deputy Carter through the attack and shooting. Channel 8 was on the scene and was asking for a statement, which I provided. Later, I wondered whether I looked as rattled as the coverage from the night of Jenni's homicide. I now understood why things appeared to be so disorganized that night. There are so many issues to be examined and discussed. I had to make on-the-fly decisions about what could be shared and what could not.

Later that afternoon after we had returned to the office, I instructed Deputy Carter, "Contact Sheriff Matthews in Twain County and ask if any of Jake

Cummings' family drives a two-tone brown 1996 Ford Club cab pickup."

It was only a few minutes later when Deputy Carter came to the office and commented that Sheriff Matthews was not aware of any family members who drove a truck by that description. She remarked, "I confirmed it was not on the list of vehicles the sheriff sent previously."

I instructed Deputy Carter, "Check the wire for any stolen vehicles by that description. Check Oklahoma and Missouri."

Yelling to the outer office, I asked Beverly, "Please check with the trauma hospital and see if they will give you a status on Deputy Allen. I need to be here following up on this. I need to write my report. But I also need to be in Tulsa checking on Deputy Allen."

I could hear Beverly reply from the outer office but did not understand what she was saying. A bit agitated, I yelled back to her, "I cannot hear you; my air is on."

As she approached my office door, she repeated, "I will be off work in about an hour. I will go to Tulsa and wait for word on Allen. I can stay the night if needed."

"That would be very helpful. Also, please call Deputy Spicer and see if he can cover Allen's shift for a while."

Deputy Carter came into my office and advised, "Sheriff, they have found what is probably the Ford truck. It was stolen from a farm outside of Joplin Missouri this morning. It has been torched just off Highway 43 south of Joplin. I suspect they stole the truck and left their vehicle somewhere close by. After they shot up your patrol car, they returned, torched the truck, and drove away in their vehicle."

"If they did all of that outside of Joplin, it would be logical to assume they are in the Joplin area, or somewhere north or east of there. My guess is northeast. About three hours northeast."

Deputy Carter asked, "Why do you think they would not be going west into Kansas?"

"I suspect this is the King family and going into Kansas would be out of their way if they were going home from Carlin County. When you are trying to leave someplace in a hurry, you would not want to waste time unnecessarily."

Deputy Carter commented, "Anybody that would attack a sheriff and deputy like that has to be crazy."

"What do you mean?" I asked.

"You would have to have mental health issues to do that," she replied.

"I see television news broadcasts every time there is a school or mass shooting in this country and the national media immediately tries to find a way to tie the shooter to a mental health issue. They do it every time. It is just logical to think that someone would have to be insane to do something like that. Assuming there must be a mental health issue helps us sleep at night. It allows us to think we would recognize a person who is capable of such acts. It allows us to feel safe that it could never be someone close to us. Mental health issues may play a part on occasion, but let me tell you, it is the evil in people that causes those types of actions. Pure unadulterated evil. Sometimes it seems as though evil is carried by the wind and blows into the least likely of places, leaving no town or neighborhood immune from it. Evil exists in every town and in every neighborhood, and so does the violence that accompanies it."

"I have never thought of it that way, but sometimes people do have mental issues that impact their behavior and lead to violence," she replied.

"Yes, that happens, but I believe it is more often related to the evil in people's hearts and minds. My grandfather told me, "Will, do not make your shade under the tree of evil." Carter, some folks do. Boy, I got on my stump for that one, didn't I?"

With a sheepish grin, Carter replied, "Yes Sir."

Later that evening, Beverly called and advised, "Deputy Allen is in intensive care at Tulsa Regional Trauma. He was in surgery for four and a half hours but is alive. The Doctor said he is stable, but this is going to be a long road for Deputy Allen."

"Are you going to stay the night?" I asked.

"Yes, I think that would be best. They recovered a .22 caliber round from Allen. The Doctor said if it had been a larger caliber weapon, we would be planning a funeral instead of Allen's recovery. She said Allen may wake up by tomorrow and I'd like to be here to let him know we are praying for him. I will need to leave early in the morning to get to the office. Maybe when I leave someone else can be here for a while?"

"I will talk to Shelley about keeping James and Jenni and I will be there."

Typically, I did not have a difficult time getting a good night's sleep. But that night, knowing that someone had the fortitude to execute an attack like that, and I had a deputy lying in intensive care in a trauma hospital, sleep was elusive. Thoughts about the violence of that act, the sound of the bullets hitting my patrol car, the shattering glass, and the image of Allen's lifeless eyes, raced through my mind and allowed me no peace.

I was in the office well before sunrise the next morning. I may have been dependent on coffee to keep me moving, but I was there. I knew I was going to have a long day with a trip to Tulsa and I needed to get the investigation of yesterday's events underway.

When Carter and Kingfisher arrived at the office, I conducted our morning meeting. The first objective for the day was the continued security and integrity of the crime scene. I was placing that responsibility on their shoulders. Also, they were to continue the search for shell casings along the roadway.

It was nearly seven o'clock when I left for the hospital. I hoped to arrive by eight-thirty and maybe be present when the doctor visited Deputy Allen during morning rounds.

As the nurse walked me into Allen's room she commented, "Your deputy is doing well, but he has a long road ahead of him. He has been drifting in and out of consciousness this morning, so do not be surprised if he is not responsive to you. If we see any signs of distress from him, we will come in and ask you to leave.

"Thank you, ma'am," I replied.

When I entered the room, I paused momentarily beside Allen's bed. Standing by his bed looking down at his motionless body stirred a rage in me. I told myself, 'The people who did this will endure our pursuit and punishment. They will pay a price for what they have done.'

Eventually, I took a seat in a well-aged tan vinyl chair beside Allen's bed. He had a myriad of lines and tubes running to different pieces of equipment in the room. The beeping tone of the EKG pierced the otherwise silent room. He appeared to be asleep, so I thought I would just sit quietly for a while. Although this was not a position I was familiar with and had no idea of the things you are supposed to say, eventually I began to speak. "Allen, the doctor said you are going to be alright. You will make a full recovery. Do not worry about anything. One of us will stop by your house once or twice every day to check on your family. We will make sure your livestock is taken care of as well. You put all your energy into getting better."

I seemed to run out of words to say and fell silent for a while. I sat and watched the EKG flash its sharp peaks across the grid on the screen as the beep continued with every heartbeat. I was so thankful that his heart was still beating.

Eventually, I mustered a few additional words. "We are going to miss having you around the office for a while. You decide when you want to return to work and let me know. We will wait for you. I will find a way to get back up here and visit again. Tell April that if she needs anything, all she needs to do is let us know. It will be taken care of. We want your family to have time to be here with you as much as possible."

The one-way conversation took all of ten minutes and made me very uncomfortable. I realized that I lacked comforting words and was not a good person to have around in a situation like this. It was not long before I began to fidget and was shuffling around in my chair. Although I felt guilty for leaving Allen lying there in bed, after an hour or so of uncomfortable silence, I rose from my seat and left Allen's room. As I passed by the Nurse's station, I asked the nurse to please tell Deputy Allen that I had been by to see him. I want him to know I was here.

While in Tulsa I contacted Director Simmons at the Oklahoma State Bureau of Investigation. I described the attack on Allen and myself to the Director and asked for assistance in conducting the investigation. I explained, "Director Simmons, I am afraid this type of crime and the resulting investigation are beyond my skillset at this point. This is a bit over my head. My deputies have been around for a while, but this is beyond their experience as well. If you are available to help us, we need all the help the OSBI can provide."

"Sheriff Rogers, "We were aware of the shooting and were in the process of determining availability and assigning agents. Contacting you was high on my list for this morning. I was about to give you a call. A couple of agents and I will be available whenever you want to get started."

"I would like to get started as soon as possible. Today is not too soon," I replied.

"It will take us a few hours to get there, but we should be at your office by two o'clock this afternoon. If you would send written statements, photos, and any information you have up to this point, my agents will review everything while we are on the road."

"You will receive everything we have in an email in a matter of minutes. Thank you. We will see you at two o'clock."

Traffic issues and road construction delayed their arrival, but they were in my office later that afternoon. "Director Simmons, it is good to meet you. These are two of our Carlin County deputies, Carter and Kingfisher. Carter led the investigation into a robbery at a local liquor store. She and Kingfisher made quick work of the investigation and subsequent arrest. Who knows when we will get the guy into the courtroom, but he will stay in jail until then."

We completed the introductions, including OSBI agents, Stephens and Carlson.

"If you received the email from Deputy Carter, you have everything we know at this point. We were just discussing how we locate and question the owner of the Ford pickup. Them being in Missouri slows that down somewhat."

The Director explained, "That is where the OSBI offers benefits. We bring resources and experience to an investigation, and we have the necessary relationships across state lines that county law enforcement typically does not have. Interstate crimes and cross-jurisdictional issues are something we deal with every day."

Agent Carlson commented, "We are here to support rural counties. We realize that, unlike larger, more populated counties, rural counties simply do not typically have the manpower necessary to conduct investigations like this. Let me be clear, we understand it is a manpower issue, not necessarily a knowledge or ability issue."

Agent Stephens added, "We contacted the Newton County Sheriff's office this afternoon while en route. They have retrieved the VIN from the truck and are investigating the owner."

"Thank you," I replied. "I have a request. I do not know what is permitted, but I would appreciate it if you could let my deputies shadow your agents. They will have the opportunity to see and learn things they are not normally exposed to. Even doing leg work for you would be a good experience for them. What they learn would no doubt benefit this department in the future."

The Director replied, "Yes, we will keep your deputies involved in aspects of the investigation that are in Carlin County. If we make a connection across state lines, the FBI may decide to get involved. That will be their call though."

Agent Carlson looked across the table and asked, "Sheriff, were you able to see the suspects? Can you identify them?"

"No, I did not get a good look at them," I replied.

Agent Carlson continued, "Do you have any thoughts on who this could be? Is there anybody that would want to do harm to you or any of your deputies?"

"I do not know if you were agents then, but do you remember the Jenni Whittington murder up on Route 66? Do you remember the shooting involving county deputies and Jake Cummings?" They nodded their confirmation.

I continued, "Well, Jake and I had a history and I suspect his family believed I had something to do with his death. He had visited my house prior to being shot by the deputies. Also, James King, the guy in jail for the liquor store robbery is Jake Cummings' son."

Deputy Carter commented, "We strongly believe the robbery was a setup to get the sheriff into the store to assault and possibly even kill him."

I added, "King has expressed to me his regrets for not finishing the job. He also told me his family would keep coming after me until they got the job done. We believe it is more of Jake Cummings' family. I think they are trying to make good on King's promise. So, to answer your question, yes, there are some folks who would like to see me harmed. We suspect they were after me, not Deputy Allen."

Agent Carlson replied, "Yes, we remember that case and that shooting. We reviewed the records of the homicide investigation and the shooting by the deputies thoroughly back then."

I commented, "My deputies and I have discussed it, and we cannot think of anybody from this area that has that serious of a grudge against us."

Deputy Carter added, "Nobody dislikes any of us that much."

Director Simmons asked, "I assume our agents will have the same office space and resources available as last time?

Deputy Carter replied, "Yes, just down the hall."

Director Simmons added, "We will get the investigation underway. Sheriff Rogers, we will provide routine updates on the investigation for you and your deputies. Any thoughts you have on the investigation, or any information you have, please share with agents Stephens and Carlson. You and your deputies are the closest law enforcement to the case and will undoubtedly have valuable insights."

With that, we adjourned and assisted the agents as they began settling into the office they had occupied during their previous investigation years earlier. It was a small, cramped space, with only a couple of desks and one phone but it would serve its purpose. I did not recall having seen this office before that time. I was taken aback by the condition of the room. The old green paint on the walls was flaking off in several spots exposing the previous eggshell white finish, and the musty smell made it difficult for me to draw a deep breath. The dark green speckled floor tile was in great shape compared to the rest of the space. I was a little embarrassed with what we had to offer.

"Any office supplies or anything else you want or need, let one of us know. Beverly can help you as well," I explained. "We will wipe things down for you, get a fan in here, and air it out."

I looked across the room and asked Deputy Carter to hang back for a minute. As the last person was leaving the room, I told her, "Again, I have been impressed by your approach to your work and how you handled the liquor store investigation."

"Thank you," she replied.

"I want you to learn all you can from the FBI and OSBI agents during this investigation. At some point, I would like you to go through our cold case files and select a case you would like to reopen. I suspect we do not have many cold cases, but there is surely something in there you would like to work."

"Sheriff, I would love to have that opportunity."

"You will need to get other deputies involved to help run down leads and share their thoughts. You will be developing their investigative skills as well. You decide when you do it. Whenever you feel you are ready."

"Oh, I am sure they will have things to offer an investigation. Thank you, Sheriff," she replied.

"Just let me know when you find a case you want to reopen."

"It takes a lifetime to build a good reputation, but you can lose it in a minute."
– Will Rogers

Chapter Seven

As the calendar rolled to August, the days had become hotter and drier than normal. That Saturday morning was no exception. The skies were clear, and even during the early morning the thermometer still rested at eighty-three degrees. As I occupied my time waiting for James and Little Jenni to get out of bed, I walked to the creek and splashed cold water on my face. There is nothing as refreshing as that cold spring water. Water never seems as pure as when it comes straight from the spring where it flows so plentifully from the earth below. The creek was running strong for August and the water level was higher than I remembered from years past. Recent events motivated me to discuss some things with James and Little Jenni. I decided this would be a good day to walk with them.

After breakfast, I asked them to walk with me for a while. As usual, we began our walk just west of the barn and began walking northward along the creek. Today the conversation would not be about Jenni or the time we spent together there. They are still young, but it was time James and Little Jenni began to understand that more happens on our walks than simple storytelling.

As we walked, I explained, "When we walk you listen to me tell stories about your mom. Occasionally, I will tell you stories from my childhood. Today I will begin teaching you the other things that happen while we walk."

"What do you mean?" James asked.

"When we walk, like we are today, you listen to me tell stories. While I talk, I am also looking at things in our environment. I am looking at the plants and grasses. I am looking at the water. I am looking at the animals, like rabbits, squirrels, and deer. I am looking at the trees. All these things tell a story as well. They tell me about the health of our environment and the land."

Little Jenni replied, "I have not seen any squirrels."

"That is because you have not learned to see them. What you know at this point is to listen as I speak, and to watch the path in front of you. As you grow and get older you will learn to see beyond the path in front of you. But another thing you will learn is to remember the path behind you. Because in life, what lies in the past is important just like what lies ahead." I became quiet to allow them to consider that for a moment.

After a few minutes I continued, "You said you have not seen any squirrels. I have seen five already. I have seen wild ginger, wild grapes, huckleberry bushes, and some young sassafras. These things tell us the land is healthy. It will provide many things in the coming seasons. These were lessons taught by generations of our ancestors. My father and grandfather taught these things to me like their fathers and grandfathers taught them. I will teach them to you."

"Maybe the most important lesson I have to offer you is a little harder to understand, but I need to teach you and let you begin to determine how the message will impact you. It is something that you will come to better understand as you get older."

"I will tell you the story as it was told to me."

"My grandfather and I walked along this same creek when I was seven years old. As we walked, my grandfather asked me a simple question, "How many directions are there?"

"After thinking about his question, I replied, "That is easy Grandpa, there are four directions, north, south, east, and west."

"As we continued to walk, he asked, "What about up and down, above and below?"

"Again, I thought for a few seconds and replied enthusiastically, "Then there are six directions."

"We continued to walk for a minute and my grandfather stopped, looked at me, and said, "There are seven directions."

"Not quite understanding how he had identified six directions but now said there are seven, I was confused. I looked up into his eyes and asked, "How can there be seven directions?"

"While pointing toward his chest, he calmly and solemnly replied, "The seventh direction lies within you. Your seventh direction defines who you are. Your relationship with the world around you is determined by your seventh direction. It determines how you interact with people and respond to things that people do."

Little Jenni replied, "I do not understand."

I continued, "The point is that you, and only you, are responsible for how you interact with the world around you and the decisions you make. It is easy to blame others for the things you do when they turn out badly. It takes a person with strength of character to take responsibility for their actions. They have a strong seventh direction."

As we walked, I continued, "Honor, courage, and kindness come from the seventh direction, but so do dishonor, cowardice, and evil."

James replied, "I think I understand."

"Everybody has a seventh direction, and each of us is responsible for ourselves. Being young, it is a hard thing to understand, but we will discuss it many times as you get older. Trust me, it will make sense to you someday. Whenever you have questions, ask me. I can tell you what the seventh direction means to me, but you must learn and decide what it means to you."

As we continued our walk that day, I began teaching them about the different trees and wild plants that are so abundant on our farm.

As we began our walk back to the house, I stopped, looked at Little Jenni, and commented, "You are almost the same age I was when my grandfather had that conversation with me. He realized I would soon become a young man and had decided I was old enough to begin learning the lessons of our ancestors. Like then, I realize you will soon become a young lady. With that in mind, I think we should stop calling you Little Jenni. Your mother was one of the best people we will ever know, but you will soon step out of her shadow and become a strong, independent young woman. We should recognize that and call you by your name, Jenni."

She looked at me with that special, precious face that indicated she was not quite sure what to say and replied, "Okay."

With a grin, I asked her, "When you get married someday, we do not want the Preacher to say, "Harold, do you take Little Jenni to be your wife?" do we?" James and I laughed.

I enjoyed our walk that day and understood we would need many discussions in the future. But I was determined to raise them with an appreciation of the gifts we are given every day and an understanding of being a good and honorable person.

When we were nearly home, I could see Shelley's car in the driveway. As we entered the house Shelley commented, "We thought we would stop by for a surprise visit."

In unison, Shelley, Mary, and Madison yelled, "Surprise!"

Shelley commented, "The girls wanted to go swimming, and I thought a swim in the creek would be good for them. So here we are."

"I am glad you came. I am sure James and Jenni would enjoy a swim as well and I wanted to discuss something with you," I replied.

"You have been preoccupied recently. What is on your mind?"

As we walked to the creek with the kids, I replied, "You know maybe I am not the best at this relationship thing, but I am enjoying the time I spend with you. I have been married twice and could not make it work either time. In my defense, the last time was during a drunken period. Maybe it is because we are older, but this is different. We have a different kind of relationship than any I have been in before."

"It makes me happy to hear that. I agree."

I explained, "I feel closer to you than anybody I have ever known. I am more comfortable than I have ever been. I am more trusting than ever before. And I just said more about a relationship than ever before." We both laughed.

We sat on the creek bank and watched the children splash and play in the water. I became distracted as I thought back on the summers that I played with my brothers and friends in the same swimming hole. There is nothing in this world that feels as refreshing as the cold spring water as it flows across your skin in the hot summer sun. We often visited the creek to refresh ourselves after a long day working in the field.

"Things are different for me as well," she replied.

I continued, "But the deeper and stronger my feelings get, the more concerned I am about the safety of you, Mary, Madison, James, and Jenni. The threats from Jake Cummings' family are real and it concerns me. I fear that folks who are that evil do not play by rules that have limits. Jake was evil. He had been since we were children. He could have come to the house and told me he had nothing to do with Jenni's murder. We could have talked it through. But instead, he chose to sneak to the house under the cover of darkness, armed, and willing to resort to violence. I am sure it was in some part because of a spat we had at a high school keg party over twenty years prior. And it appears his son and family share that same degree of evil. I am new at this, and I am not sure I know how to protect you and the kids. I think I might feel better if you and the kids were all in one place. I can have patrols come by and we can stay in close contact on the phone when I am working."

"Will, are you asking me to move in with you?"

"Yes. Would that be a bad thing?"

"I do not know that it would be a bad thing, but it would certainly be a change for everybody. It would make things a lot easier for taking care of James and Jenni though. You would not need to drive all the way to my house every day to pick them up. They would already be home. That would actually make things easier for all of us."

"But would it be the best thing for you and the girls? Your life is uncomplicated now."

"Trust me, my life is a bit more complicated than you realize. I guess one thing we need to consider and think about is the conditions of that move.

The Sheriff of Carlin County

Would it be platonic, or would it be the next level of our relationship?" she asked.

I replied, "It would be easy to say it would be platonic, but I know if you are in the same house as me, asking for something more is going to be easy. That is unavoidable. For me, it would be the next level of our relationship. Are the girls ready to see that happen? Are you ready to see that happen?"

"I agree that it would be the next step for us, and I am ready for that, but that would not be a step, that would be a leap."

I asked her, "Do you think the girls are ready to see you share my bed?"

"Let's not kid ourselves. I think the girls already know I have been in your bed, and you have been in mine. Kids these days are a little smarter and not quite as naive as we were."

"Do we try a weekend and see how it goes?" I asked.

She replied, "I think that would be the smartest thing to do. Maybe we can ease into it. After the first weekend, I can talk to the girls and see if there are any issues."

"You tell me when. I will clear out the extra bedroom. I can put all my stuff in the barn for now. I'll have to get another bed for the girls though."

She replied, "Two weeks from now. Does that give you time to move your stuff? The girls can sleep on the floor or on an air mattress for a weekend. Do not worry about another bed for them yet."

"I am sure I can get it done. Two weeks it is."

She laughed as she said, "Poor James. He will be sharing a bathroom with three girls. Before we do this, are you sure you want to deal with the drama of three young girls? You routinely hear my tales of woe, but living it is something different entirely."

"If I can handle the drama at the sheriff's office, I can handle three young girls – I think."

*"Even if you are on the right track,
you will get run over if you just sit there."*
– Will Rogers

Chapter Eight

"Good morning, Sheriff," Agent Stephens said as he walked through my office door. "I scheduled this time with you to discuss the investigation into the shooting of Deputy Allen. As we said previously, we will have routine meetings to keep you informed on our progress."

"I definitely appreciate any details you share with us."

"So far, we are pleased with how it is progressing. Because we suspect Jake Cummings' family is involved and the fact that they would have crossed state lines, the FBI is joining the investigation. They have resources for investigating multi-jurisdictional crimes and their surveillance of suspects is second to none."

He continued, "I just received word that the Newton County Sheriff has sent a description of a car left in the area of the stolen Ford pickup truck to the FBI and OSBI."

"It isn't a small light blue sedan is it?" I asked.

"Actually I have not seen the description at this point, but I should be receiving it anytime now. Is there something meaningful about that vehicle?" he asked.

"Well, there could be. The liquor store robbery suspects were driving a small light blue sedan. I believed it was Jake Cummings' car that was picked up from our impound yard by James King but is registered to his half-brother, Rodney Rickert."

He replied, "I will let you know as soon as I get the information."

He continued, "FBI agents have begun their surveillance of the family members Sheriff Matthews identified as being most likely to be involved."

"How are they surveilling? Is it monitoring cell phone traffic or physical observation?" I asked.

Agent Stephens replied, "Sheriff, for now, it may be best to just let them do what they do and reap the benefits. Do not worry about how it happens. The FBI gets results. When this is over, we will talk."

He continued, "We are handling working with Joplin area authorities and the Missouri State Police, the FBI will handle everything in the Twain County area with the sheriff up there. We can already tell you that your hunch about their involvement appears to be accurate. There is a lot of activity up there with that family."

As we were about to conclude our meeting, Agent Stephens received a text message with the vehicle description. He commented, "Sheriff, the vehicle was not the light blue sedan you mentioned."

True to his commitment, we met again a few days later for another update.

He began, "Regarding details on the vehicle, a Newton County Sheriff's Deputy was patrolling that area the morning of the attack on you and Deputy Allen. He noticed the vehicle parked on the shoulder of a side road and assumed it was a disabled vehicle, made a note of the license plate number, and placed a 'Notification to Remove' sticker on the window. It was not registered to Rodney Rickert. It was a small gray sedan registered to Kimberly King. She is James King's mother. They have interviewed Ms. King. She now claims the vehicle was stolen sometime during the night prior to it being parked in Newton County. She stated she had not had time to report it to the authorities. Minutes before I got here this morning, Missouri State Police found the vehicle. It was located outside St. James Missouri. Of course, it had been burned."

"That is quite telling that the vehicle is from up there, parked down here, and then returned to St. James, isn't it?" I asked.

"In our opinion, there is no doubt that whoever was driving that car was somehow involved in the shooting of your deputy. How is he doing by the way?" he asked.

"He is getting better every day. They say he should make a full recovery. We hope to get him back on office duty soon."

He continued, "We have combed the scene of the attack. We collected a couple of shell casings that had not been flagged. As you know we searched your patrol car. We reviewed all the evidence your deputies marked and collected. We also recovered shell casings from the Ford pickup. We can say a 9mm and based on the number of casings, probably two .22 caliber weapons were used. It is a bit surprising they would use .22 caliber weapons. But if the family up there are trappers, we would not be surprised to see that small caliber handguns and rifles are what they would own and have most readily available."

"Yeah, that makes sense."

"Ms. King is clearly nervous, but we do not think she will ever give up a family member. Those are the important details. Oh, by the way, you are quite popular up there. Not well-liked, but well known. There are a lot of folks up there that know who you are. They call you, 'the Okie'. The FBI heard some chatter about a scuffle between you and Jake Cummings."

"Yeah, we had a little episode. That was over twenty years ago at a high school keg party. Jake did not win that night. He was a bit too drunk to be fighting, and I think he realized it was not going to be a good night if he continued to push the issue. I have assumed that is why he came to my house looking for a fight the night he was shot and killed by county deputies."

"Sheriff Rogers, we do not think it will take long for a member of the family to make a mistake. Missouri State Police and the FBI will continue interviewing family members and applying pressure. At some point, someone will break and give up the details."

I commented, "If they haven't met with the cashier from our liquor store robbery, I think he may be a soft spot. If the car was torched in St. James, there is some chance he may have information. He left here and returned home fleeing the investigation into the liquor store robbery. I am confident he will get nervous and uncomfortable when the FBI starts talking about charges for attempted murder of a peace officer."

Agent Stephens replied, "I will make sure they have his name. We will place him in their sights."

"As nervous as he was when Deputies Carter and Kingfisher interviewed him the third or fourth time, I do not think he will be able to endure being interviewed by the FBI. They made him nervous enough that he rabbited back to St. James."

"Don't let yesterday take up too much of today"
– **Will Rogers**

Chapter Nine

Of course, two weeks rolled around quickly, but I thought James, Jenni, and I were prepared for our weekend visitors.

Mary and Madison rode the school bus home with James and Jenni. Shelley arrived at the house a few minutes ahead of me. So, when I arrived, the house was bustling with activity. Everybody was getting ready to leave for the first high school football game of the season. With this being a new thing for all involved and wanting to keep things simple, I suggested we go to the local pizza place for dinner before the game.

Following the game, we returned to the farm, turned on the television, and relaxed for a while. I could see Shelley as she watched me to see how I was coping with having so many bodies in the house.

I smiled as I told her, "Hey, I am going to be alright. This is not that bad."

As she replied, "How did you know I...," I interrupted her and commented, "All is good with me. I just discovered that so much of what we hear is the sound of laughter, and the sound of relationships growing. I have never heard James and Jenni laugh so much or so hard. That makes me happy. I just have to learn to protect it. I want these kids to grow up in a safe place."

The following morning, I was first to the kitchen. I put on a pot of coffee and headed to the shower. By the time I had my shower, dressed, and returned to the kitchen, everybody was up except Jenni. I told James, "Give her twenty to thirty more minutes, then you may get her up. It will be time for breakfast."

As I prepared my cup of coffee and leaned against the counter, Shelley placed her arms around my neck and kissed me. I was a little surprised and she clearly sensed my hesitancy. She said, "I am not going to be shy about showing my affection in front of the children. If this is what we are going to do, that will be a part of it."

I replied, "I am good with that," as I watched the kids to see if there was any reaction. They were oblivious to us. It was as if we were not in the room.

I told Shelley, "I think they are comfortable with us. You may do that again."

James, Jenni, and I sat at our little table every morning to have breakfast together. The little table was a bit crowded today. I grimaced as I told Shelley, "Oops, I did not think about the size of our little table."

"We will manage," she replied.

"James, join me at the counter and let Shelley have your seat. You should always give up your seat for an elder or a lady. We will let the girls sit at the table."

After the kids had left the table and Shelley and I were relaxing and enjoying our coffee, I commented, "The last time I saw Jenni, we sat at her table much like we are doing now, relaxing and enjoying a cup of coffee. Now when I think back, she knew at that time James was my son, and she had to be debating telling me and I had no idea. Now I am sitting with you not having a clue what is going through your mind. Are you thinking of things that could have a profound impact on my life? Or are you thinking you should have added more salt to the potatoes?"

As she pointed to her head, she said, "There is actually very little going on in there." We both burst into laughter. "Actually, I am thinking about how comfortable I am. Being with you is relaxing.

It is just natural for me. I can be myself and not constantly think about everything that is going on around us. I can be myself and know that I am accepted for that. I know you will protect us and my children are safe. You've been out there for years and I missed it. I want to make up for that lost time."

"That was deep. I agree and feel the same way. But do not look back with regret at what we have missed. Think about what we can do for those four kids. But you have to remember, I am a guy with some baggage. There will be demons surface from my past that I will have to deal with. And we both know this job will bring about more issues, even things that will creep into our personal lives."

"You think you are a big, mean, grumpy old bear, but you are a kind, generous man with a comforting soul."

"Okay, let's stop talking about me. I need to check the cows. Do you want to ride along?" I asked.

"I need to get a few things done here in the house. Are you riding a horse or a four-wheeler? Actually, it does not matter, I know Madison would love to go with you. Would you mind?" she asked.

"I think that would be great."

Shelley yelled to the other room, "Madison, come here for a second. Would you like to ride with Will to check the cows?"

"Yes," she answered.

I asked Madison, "Would you rather ride a horse or a four-wheeler?"

Excited, she replied, "Can we ride a horse?"

I replied, "Yes ma'am, we certainly can. Run and get ready and I will meet you at the barn. I will go saddle the buckskin, Ginger."

As we rode along the creek, I asked her, "Are you enjoying being here at the farm?"

"Yeah, but it is quiet. And it was really dark last night. It was kind of scary."

"It is quiet, and it certainly does get dark out here with no streetlights. But a person gets used to it."

As we arrived at the first pasture, I told her, "There should be fifty-two cows in this field. Can you help me count them?"

A moment later I verified the count and asked her how many she counted. "I cannot count them. They keep moving. They need to stop moving."

From there we rode to another pasture. I told Madison, "There should be 27 cows in this field. You want to try counting again?"

"I will try," she replied.

Like before, I finished counting them and asked if she had finished. "I count 29," she answered.

"Well, you are getting better. I guess it is something you learn to do. Have you ever ridden a horse before?"

"No," she replied.

"Would you like to?"

"Yeah," she replied. "But what if I mess up?"

"I'll be right here to help you."

I sat her in the saddle and took my place behind her. I explained how to hold the reins and how to let the horse know when you want to go right or left or want to stop. And most importantly, that you control the horse's speed by how much rein you give them.

"Okay. Take us home," I told her.

Other than the times she gave too much rein and we and Ginger galloped, bouncing Madison in the saddle, she did well on the ride back to the barn. As we arrived at the barn, she pulled back on the reins and Ginger stopped just outside the barn door.

As I took the reins from her, I told her she did a great job. "If you want to ride again sometime just let me know. When you get used to riding, and Ginger gets used to you, you will be able to ride by yourself."

"That would be awesome!" She started running toward the house while screaming, "Mom, I drove a horse." She would spend much of the rest of the day running around the yard with her hands extended like she was holding reins and saying, "Giddy up, Ginger, giddy up."

That afternoon, James, Jenni, Mary, and Madison asked if we could have a bonfire that night. Mary said, "You know, like we did that night we came to your house and rode behind the tractor. I really liked sitting by the fire."

"If your mom does not have other plans, we can do that. We will have to gather some wood for the fire though. Do you want to have hot dogs like we did that night?" I asked.

Mary replied, "Yes," while the other three children nodded their approval of the idea.

"Do you mind if I invite some friends?" I asked. I have not been able to spend time with them in a while and it would be good to see them. You might remember them from the hayride. It is Josh and Amy."

Madison asked, "Was she the lady who rode in the trailer with us?"

"Yes," I replied.

"I liked her. She was fun."

"Mary, before you take off to gather firewood, I want to ask you something. Have you ever driven a car?"

She replied, "Sometimes mom lets me pull the car into the driveway."

"But you have never driven beyond that? There is a good place along the creek to gather some kindling for the fire. You may drive my old truck down there if you would like."

"What about mom?" she asked.

"I have already spoken with your mom and she is fine with you driving in the field. It is one of the perks of living on a farm."

"Really?" she asked.

As I pulled the keys from my pocket and handed them to her, I replied, "Yes."

She did not appear to be nervous as she backed the old truck from the driveway and drove into the field.

We gathered wood for the fire and returned to the house. I told her, "You did great. We will let you bring the truck into the field from time to time to continue practicing. By the time driver's education starts you will be ready."

That evening as we started our bonfire and took our seats around the fire pit, I shared the same seventh-direction discussion I'd had with James and Jenni.

Not long after dinner, the kids began migrating back to the house to play video games. I appreciated that the adults had some time to talk.

It only took a minute and Amy began to speak. She commented, "Will, we have been so worried about you. The violent incidents you have endured are concerning."

"Oh, do not worry about me. Those are just things that go with the job."

She replied sharply, "Do not try to snow me, I know that is not normal."

"You know I appreciate your concern, but I am going to be okay. When Joe asked me to serve the balance of his term, my first reaction was a solid 'No'. But I thought about it for a few days and realized that maybe I was selling myself short. I automatically assumed that I had nothing to offer in that role. I am beginning to realize that I can do the job and possibly help folks have better lives. Or, at least, safer lives.

Josh replied, "That all sounds wonderful, but I must ask, "What have you done with my friend Will?"

"It is still me, Buddy. Maybe just being sober is not all I have to offer or accomplish. I am learning to like this job and I think I truly do have something to offer."

Josh replied, "Do not misunderstand me, I am not putting down your choice. I think it is tremendous that you have stepped out of your comfortable, routine life. But you have been in situations where you could have been seriously hurt or even died."

"Maybe having an opportunity to make a difference in people's lives is worth that risk. Like I said, I am actually starting to like this job. The funny thing is that as you know I am not a social person, but the interaction with folks is the part I am enjoying."

"That is a surprise," Amy commented.

I replied, "I am happy you are here, and I hope the four of us can spend more time together."

Amy asked, "So, are you guys becoming an item?"

Shelley jumped into the conversation and replied, "Yes. If he has never told you, I was in love with him when he was a senior in high school. Through James and Jenni's adoption process, I got to see that he is a strong, kind, and generous man. My girlhood crush was rekindled, and here we are."

I added, "It looks that way. She understands me and sees past my unpolished nature. She knows I have demons and can be rough around the edges. She does not hold my old ways against me."

At the end of the evening, as we walked along the pathway to the house, Shelley commented, "The seventh direction discussion was a philosophical side of you I never knew about. If you help me understand, I can help educate the girls. But I have to ask, why the full-court press on the life lessons with the kids?"

"I have only been interim sheriff for a few months and have already been clubbed over the head and shot at. I now understand that if I am in this job longer term, how long I roam these old county roads is not guaranteed. It is important to me for the kids to understand some simple things that may help them be better people. I guess I have always felt I had a long life ahead of me to share the things I have learned about my ancestors. Having already been through two assaults that could have snuffed my candle, I realize life is not guaranteed, and if I am going to share these things, I need to get to it."

I asked, "Are we going to do this again next week?"

"Yes, I think it worked out well. Maybe even better than I had hoped," she replied with a broad smile. "The girls will be telling their friends about it for days. Mary got to drive your truck, and Madison drove a horse," she said with a smile. "I hope you know you have made their weekend."

"Some people try to turn back their odometers. Not me, I want people to know "why" I look this way. I've traveled a long way and some of the roads weren't paved."
– Will Rogers

Chapter Ten

I have never been a person to do anything special on my birthday, but it had been a busy time and I decided to take a couple of hours for myself. James and Jenni would be going to Shelley's house after school with the girls, and I would have a little time to relax and catch my breath. I left the office and drove home. As I pulled into the driveway, I could see Joe's Chevy pickup parked behind the barn. I was glad to see that he was there and was anxious to tell him how things had been going around the office. He had visited several times since he had originally mentioned occasional visits when he told me about his cancer. I parked my patrol car and walked past the barn and to Joe's favorite spot by the bend in the creek. I could see Joe sitting in a chair he kept there for his visits. Not wanting to startle him, I called his name as I walked toward his chair. He did not respond. I called out his name again as I reached out and placed my hand on his shoulder. He did not move. My heart raced as my mind began running through the possible scenarios of why he did not respond. I hesitated and drew a deep breath. "Hey, my friend. Are you okay?" I asked.

Again, no response. I stepped in front of him and knelt down. I could not see any movement in his chest. I placed my fingers on his neck to check his pulse. There was no pulse. His skin was cool to the touch. I reached up with my left hand and gently closed his eyes. I knew I had just lost one of the dearest friends I would have in my lifetime. I knew I would miss him and our talks, but I took some comfort in knowing that his pain was gone. I smiled thinking back on the conversation when he talked about this special place on the creek and him finding his peace here. I sat for a while and talked to him. I told him how things were going at the office. I told him the kids were going to miss him and his visits. I told him goodbye in the way a man of honor deserved.

There was a small wooden box in Joe's lap containing a small amount of tobacco. Joe had visited the medicine man in Tall Tree as we had discussed. The medicine man was not able to offer much beyond the tobacco but explained to Joe that he would leave this life and begin a new journey.

The tobacco would help him find peace with the transition.

I paused for a moment to offer a simple prayer for Joe.

I was certain that some folks would find my approach a bit odd, but I was in no hurry to turn Joe over to the coroner. I saw no reason to hurry the process. Many times in my life I wished I'd had just a few minutes alone with my parents when they died. There were things I would like to have said before they were taken away. I wished I had told them goodbye.

I pulled my phone from my pocket and called the county Dispatcher. I explained that I needed the county coroner and why. I requested she make the call without it being broadcast over the radio. "Joe deserves to do this without attracting attention. Send Deputy Carter as soon as she can get here. Tell the coroner I will call her when we are ready for her."

Deputy Carter arrived within ten minutes. I asked her to sit with Joe while I made the drive to Joe and Betty's house to notify her. I would rather have taken a beating than make that drive and have that conversation. I knocked on the door and waited, fidgeting. She opened the door and invited me in, "Come in Will. Joe is not home." It was with the words, 'Joe is not home,' she anticipated my reason for being there.

"It is Joe, isn't it?" she asked.

"Betty, it breaks my heart to say this, but yes, it is Joe."

"Is he gone?" she asked.

"Yes. He was at the house sitting by the creek. I want to give you a chance to see him before they come to pick him up. We can go now, or you can wait and see him later."

"No, I want to see him now. Let me grab my pocketbook. I will be right back."

As we made the drive to the farm, I did not know whether she would want to talk or not, so, I let Betty carry any conversation she wanted to have.

"Will, I would like to have been by his side, but he was where he wanted to be. When we left your house the evening of the hayride, he talked about the comfort he felt there. After he asked you about coming to your farm and his first visit alone, he talked about it. He said he had never seen a place that made him feel such comfort and peace. I think the fact that it is yours made it even more special to him. I even went there with him once. We placed our chairs next to each other and sat holding hands for almost two hours. Joe talked about the things he had accomplished in life. And he talked about the things he had never done. He shared things he wanted me to tell the kids and grandkids after he was gone. I thank you for allowing him to have his time alone. With his time spent here and time at the church talking to the Pastor, I know he found the peace he had hoped for."

When we arrived at the farm, I walked with Betty to Joe's special place by the creek. She walked to Joe's chair and knelt down beside him. Deputy Carter moved another chair so Betty could sit next to him.

I told her, "Betty, we will be nearby. You let us know when you are ready, and I will call the coroner. Take as much time as you need."

As Deputy Carter and I walked away, I could hear her speaking to Joe.

While we waited for Betty to have her time with Joe, I took the opportunity to discuss something with Deputy Carter that had been on my mind for a while.

"Carter, if the liquor store robbery happened inside city limits, why did the person who reported the robbery call county dispatch and not city dispatch?" I asked.

"I never thought about it," she replied.

"That has been bothering me. I should say it has been haunting me. Maybe it is nothing, but that gut feeling that it means something will not go away. Ponder on that and let me know what you think."

We paused for a second peering back at Betty as she sat with Joe. I told Deputy Carter, "Look at them. I hope someday I can have what they shared over the decades. That is special."

About half an hour later, Betty commented, "You should call the coroner. Is it okay if I stay with Joe until the coroner arrives?" she asked.

"You may stay there as long as you like," I told her.

As the coroner was loading Joe into a hearse, I told Betty, "If you would like, you may stay for a while after they leave. We are in no hurry. Maybe you would enjoy a few minutes the way Joe did.

She replied, "Thank you, but I am ready to go home."

Betty and I had a quiet drive back to their place. After walking Betty to the door, she turned and said, "Will, Joe counted you as just about the best friend he had. He had tremendous respect for you and treasured your time together."

"I felt the same way about Joe. We had some good times together. We were able to talk a lot while he was training me. I am going to miss him the same as I missed my dad when he died."

"Do you have anybody to stay with you tonight? It might be good to have some noise in the house with you."

"Our daughter will be here tonight, or however long I need. Will, I need to start making phone calls."

"Make your calls. We will not release a public announcement until tomorrow to give you some time. Please let me know if you need anything."

From Joe and Betty's house, I drove to Shelley's to pick up James and Jenni.

Shelley met me at the door and welcomed me in. As soon as I stepped inside the doorway, I reached out for her, put my arms around her neck, and just stood there in an embrace.

"Bad day?" she asked.

"Yeah, I left the office early and drove home. When I got home, I noticed Joe was on one of his visits to the creek. I typically do not go back when he is there, but today I did. I was anxious to tell him about recent events with the department. Joe was sitting in his chair and when he didn't respond to my calls, I checked on him. He had passed away. I assumed quietly and peacefully."

"Oh, Will, I am sorry."

"I noticed he was dressed in a nice, pressed pair of jeans, a nice shirt, his best boots, and his cowboy hat. I think he knew this was going to be the day. I am not sure whether it is a blessing or a curse, but sometimes people seem to know when their life has run its course. Years ago, while lying in her hospital bed, my grandmother looked at my aunt and said, "Take me home. I will die today, and I want to die at home." My aunt talked to the doctor who agreed to release my grandmother from the hospital. Less than one hour after she arrived at home, she passed away. She knew her time was at an end. I think Joe knew his time was going to be today."

"Why did you leave work early?"

"It is my birthday and I thought I would sneak away and share a few minutes with my old long lost friend, solitude. It has been a while since I could just sit alone and relax. Maybe next year's birthday," I said with a chuckle. "Is that fried chicken I smell?"

She took me by the hand and walked me to the kitchen. Happy Birthday decorations adorned the wall. Shelley had cooked my favorite meal, and they had a birthday present for me. The present was a gift certificate for one night alone. Shelley and the girls would keep James and Jenni for an overnight stay, and I could have a night to myself. I looked at James and Jenni and with a laugh said, "Thank you. I will certainly be able to use this."

We enjoyed dinner, I blew out my candles, and we all ate cake. As the kids wandered off to play, I thanked Shelley for the surprise. I told her, "This could not have happened on a better day. I was thinking about it while we ate dinner and I realized I do not necessarily want to be alone. I do not feel like talking, but having all of you here was comforting. I have spent many birthdays alone. This one felt good."

"The road to success is dotted with many tempting parking spaces."
— **Will Rogers**

Chapter Eleven

It was late September 2013, and as usual, Shelley, the kids, and I attended the Friday night high school football game. The night air was cool, making it a perfect evening for football. Tonight was not just another football game though. It was a special night for Madison and Jenni. All cheerleaders from pee-wee football and the junior high cheer squad were invited to participate in a special part of the halftime show. Madison and Jenni had been attending special practices after school four days a week for the past two weeks to prepare for the show. They had spent many hours practicing together at home as well. It had been good to watch as the two shared a common goal they worked together to accomplish. It was easy to see them grow closer as they prepared for tonight.

As the cadence of drums led the high school band from the field to make room for the cheerleaders,

The Sheriff of Carlin County

Agent Stephens tapped me on the shoulder. As I turned, he said, "Sheriff Rogers, I am sorry to bother you at this time, but I want you to know you were correct. The liquor store clerk broke under questioning by the FBI. They applied a little pressure, offered him a deal on the liquor store robbery, and he started talking."

"Agent Stephens, please give me a couple of minutes. If I miss the next five minutes, I will regret it for the rest of my life. My own family will be calling me 'the Okie' if you know what I mean."

As the girls were marching from the field waving their pompoms, I turned to Agent Stephens. "That is great news. Sorry for the pause, but that was necessary."

"Do not think anything about it. I understand. I have a little cheerleader in the house as well. I am staying in town this weekend and thought I would catch a game and was hoping to see you here. I wanted to deliver the news from the investigation in person. When they interviewed the clerk, he named the three men who carried out the ambush on you and Deputy Allen. It was obvious to them he had information related to other crimes, but they did not press him on those additional matters. This gives them everything they need to start building a solid case against the three attackers. They will begin using his statements to bring folks in and start trying to get others to roll over as well."

"It always surprises me how quickly one crook will roll over on another to save their own skin," I replied.

"Yes sir, we bank on that. One additional detail the FBI has learned from the chatter up there. The family is planning to visit you again. There is a lot of chatter about you and Jake Cummings at your farm that keeps them buzzing. Because of what they are hearing, the FBI thinks they are coming to your house."

"Well, that is something that concerns me greatly. Looks like I may have to get my old tractor out."

Agent Stephens replied, "What? A tractor?"

"Sorry about that. That's an old thing. Does the FBI have any idea of when this might occur?"

"As of today, the answer is no. They do not think it is going to be in the next couple of days. But they will know when family members leave Tremont. They will know if any of them leave the county."

As I began my reply, "How do they...?" Agent Stephens cut me off and said, "Let's not concern ourselves with the how. Let's focus on the response to their arrival. Obviously, you will have a lot of support at your farm when they arrive."

"Thank you, Agent Stephens, for sharing that. I am thrilled to hear about the progress. Is there anything else?" I asked. "I need to get back to the family."

"No sir. If anything comes up, I will get in touch. The football team looks pretty good."

"It looks like it may be a special year for us. At least we hope so. We have been in a bit of a drought for some years now. Maybe this will be the year. Thanks again." We shook hands as we parted.

Because this was a special night for Madison and Jenni, we stopped at Charlie's Burger Barn for a post-game celebration.

As we sat waiting for our burgers, I explained to Shelley, "You know, when Joe asked me to do this thing, I thought I had considered everything there was to being interim sheriff. One area I did not see coming was the volume of issues folks talk to you about. Tonight, I heard about the Thompson's dog who barks too much at night. I heard about the Richardson boy parking his truck too close to the road. I heard about someone growing marijuana up by the Fain County line. It never stops. No matter what I am doing somebody wants my ear. I understand it is a part of the job, but there is never a moment of peace. I did not see that coming."

I continued, "It is funny though, during all my interactions with Sheriff Joe following Jenni's homicide, I always walked away thinking our time together was business-like, structured, and formal. Now I find myself creating that same atmosphere when I interact with people. I do not know whether that is the atmosphere I want to create, or if a more approachable demeanor would better serve my purpose. I try to be responsive during those conversations. As I told Josh and Amy, that is a part of this job I enjoy, but too often the interactions seem awkward and uncomfortable. I need to get better at that."

Only a moment later I received a call from the County Dispatcher. She asked if I was available to respond to a call. She said she thought this was an issue I would want to handle personally.

"What is the issue?" I asked.

"It is a domestic violence call. A couple began an argument at the football game that spilled over into their trip home and continued after they got home. This is a call you might want to respond to yourself."

I told Shelley to enjoy some time with the kids I needed to go to work for a little while. She looked at me and asked, "You have that look in your eyes. It is a domestic violence call, isn't it?"

As I leaned down to kiss her forehead, I replied, "Yes."

"Will, do not get yourself into trouble."

The Sheriff of Carlin County

It only took ten minutes or so to arrive at the residence from the call. I waited for someone to answer the door. A young lady I've known since she was an infant came to the door crying.

I asked, "Kacey, did you call the sheriff's office?"

"Yes sir, I did."

"Are you and your husband having problems tonight?" I asked. The mark on her cheek and her uncomfortable silence answered the question for me. As she began leading me to what appeared to be their living room, I asked, "Where is your husband?" He was sitting in a recliner but rose to his feet as I approached.

"Did you hit your wife?"

"That is none of your business," he replied.

"You are a grown man and hit your wife? I truly hope it was a one-time thing. You just lost your temper and did something you will never do again, right? I have known your wife since she was a baby. There is not a kinder and gentler person around these parts."

He interrupted and replied, "You do not understand. I saw her talking to her old boyfriend at the concession stand."

As his face took on a look of pure evil, he turned toward her and yelled, "I know she still wants him."

I asked, "Did she say she wants him?" I did not expect a reply and received none.

I turned to Kacey and asked, "Is there something between you and an old boyfriend?"

"No. He spoke to me, so I spoke to him… for about fifteen seconds."

I turned back to him and asked, "She spoke to someone for fifteen seconds and you think that makes it alright to hit her? Something tells me this is not the first time this has happened. A woman never calls the first time it happens. When they realize it is escalating and is not going to stop, is when they finally call. Calling me is a last resort."

I asked, "Kacey, do you want to leave?"

"No sir. I just cannot take being hit anymore."

"So, this is not the first time?"

She just hung her head and did not answer. I turned to him and asked, "So this is not the first time?"

"What happens in our home is none of your business," he yelled.

With that, I stared into his eyes for several seconds. The next time he opened his mouth to speak, I hit him with a left jab squarely across the mouth sending him stumbling backward and onto the floor in front of their coffee table. As he began to rise to his feet, I told him, "Until I leave this house you should stay down there. A man hitting a woman sickens me. It is something I will not ignore and let go unaddressed. You can stay down there and call it a night, or you can get up and take the beating of your life. He chose to stay on the floor, which told me everything I needed to know about him.

"One thing I just learned when your wife would not say you had hit her before is that she is afraid. She should now understand she has absolutely no reason to be afraid. If you ever lay a hand on her in violence again, I will come back. The next time I will not stop beating you until I know you will never touch her again."

"You barge into my home and assault me. You are abusing your position as sheriff. You could not do this if you weren't sheriff," he barked angrily.

"If I was not the sheriff and I walked into your house after you hit your wife, I would drag you outside and beat you unconscious. The only difference this uniform makes is constraint. Be thankful for that."

I pulled my radio from its belt clip with my left hand and extended it to him. "What is that for?" he asked.

"If you feel you have been treated unfairly, you can call and have a deputy sent out here."

He extended his hand but withdrew it.

"We are done here, right?" I asked. "I will never be called back here again, will I?"

"No sir," he replied with a near whisper.

"The place where Kacey should feel safe and secure is in her home. Instead, she lives in fear of when you are going to lose your temper and demonstrate your manhood by hitting her. Her home is probably where she feels the greatest level of fear. That stops now."

I extended my hand to help him from the floor. He grasped my hand and stood. I placed my hand on his shoulder and explained, "The next time you get angry, just stop and remember why you married Kacey in the first place. You did it because she was the love of your life. Treat her like you did the day of your wedding."

As I walked toward the door, I commented, "Find something fun to do together this weekend. Good night."

The following morning after breakfast, I told Shelley, "I want to take you to a special place on the farm. When I need time alone, I mean really alone, it is my sanctuary. There are numerous places on the farm that are calming and comforting, but this place is special. The spring is a small paradise on earth. I feel closest to nature when I am there. Not many folks know about it. In fact, at this point, I am not sure anybody other than me knows about it."

Along the ridge above the creek near the northern edge of the farm is a natural running spring.

One large gray limestone rock juts out about eight to ten feet from the hillside. The rock rests solidly on smaller limestone formations on both sides. Underneath is a small cavern with a pool of about six to eight inches of water. The cold, crystal clear water runs from the pool and into another small pool then overflows and cascades down the hill via a narrow gravel bed and into the creek below.

As we were getting near the spring and it was in sight, I explained, "During the drought and dust bowl days in the nineteen-thirties, folks from all over this part of the country came to this spring to get water. The drought was so bad that folks' wells and creeks dried up and many people had no water. But this little spring continued to flow and provide the most basic of life-sustaining elements. My grandfather always told me there is magic here. If you bring someone you like, drink the water, and spend some time and take in the natural beauty, you will fall in love. He claimed that happened to visitors during the Dust Bowl. In fact, during that period, it became known as Lovers' Spring. Many of the folks who came here for water brought food, picnicked, and spent time taking in the beauty of the area. After the Dust Bowl days and the Great Depression, he blocked the road, and eventually, people forgot the spring was here."

As we arrived at the spring, I spread a blanket on the ground, asked Shelley to have a seat, and explained, "You can sit or lay here and listen to the light trickle of the water. I promise it will take away whatever may trouble you." I took a seat beside her and placed my hand over hers.

Shelley asked, "Will, how did things go last night with the domestic violence call? You didn't go too far, did you?"

"Not in my opinion. But I do not think I will get called back there. I did some marriage counseling," I replied with a sideways grin.

"That is a relief," she replied.

"I knew this would be a good day to visit this place. Last night you said I had a look in my eyes and not to get myself into trouble. What did that mean?" I asked.

"I have noticed when you deal with or talk about domestic violence, you get a look in your eyes. It is kind of scary. Your demeanor changes. Your jawline tightens, your voice deepens, and your eyes get a meanness to them."

"I was not raised in a home with domestic violence, but by sharing Jenni's ordeal with Russell years ago, I understood its consequences. During my time as interim Sheriff that is one thing that I will not tolerate. It is something that may garner a harsh reaction from me."

The Sheriff of Carlin County

I continued, "Enough about that. I want to talk about something else."

"And what is that?" she asked.

"I think our weekends together are working well. I hope you and the girls agree."

Shelley replied, "There have been no issues outside of the normal drama that raising two girls entails. They enjoy James and Jenni. They essentially consider them as brother and sister. And, of course, you obviously see how happy I am. We love it here."

"Having you and the girls here has been good for James and Jenni. It is easy to see a change in them. They are happier and more engaged than before. I thought they were doing well while we were a family of three, but now I see a different level of happiness. If you would like to make this more permanent, I will add another bedroom and bathroom to the house for the girls."

"Will, if we do not work out, you will have a lot of house to take care of."

"If I was worried about us not working out, I would not have brought you to the spring. This is my private paradise, and, in my lifetime, I have only shared it with one other person. Even in a rural county like this, not many places remain where you can be so alone. Knowing that, why don't you slide on over here."

Shelley commented, "As for me, I am ready to take the next step. As for the girls, they love you, James, and Jenni, and they love being on the farm. We can plan to stay."

She continued, "It would be nice to have a small cabin here. It would be a great romantic getaway. I have seen pictures of small cabins online that would be perfect. It could be a place where we could relax and enjoy listening to the water as it flows down the hill."

I replied, "I have never considered having man-made structures back here, but if you want, we may figure out something. You are right though. It would be nice to have a shelter so we could stay here overnight."

After a few minutes of silence, I asked, "Do you remember OSBI Agent Stephens talking to me at the football game last night? He provided an update on the King family. The FBI thinks the family is still planning another visit to do me harm."

"Oh no, Will. Tell me that bunch isn't coming to the house. If so, the kids and I can stay at my place for a while," she replied.

"I have thought about that, but then I would not be with you. I assume the King family knows about you and may know where you live. I want you close so I can protect you."

"The FBI will know when the family is en route and will let us know. You will need to round up the kids and go to the courthouse."

"Will, before we go back to the house, I need to tell you something."

"Before you do that, do you agree it is time to discuss the King family situation with the kids? They need to be vigilant, and they need to know. I do not like the idea of disclosing the danger to them, but they must know. I am not comfortable exposing young kids to the reality of how harsh and violent the world is, but they need to pay attention when they are away from the house."

'Yes, I agree."

"Okay, what do you need to talk about?" I asked.

"As you know, CPS is working on a case involving the son of Steph McGee. We have temporary custody of him while we are investigating his home situation. A couple of days after we took his son, Steph began following me in his car. At first, I thought maybe it was my imagination or coincidence, but he shows up too often for it to be by chance. He even followed me part of the way home yesterday evening."

"And you are just now telling me? I will have a discussion with him."

"Will, do not get yourself into trouble."

"Never," I replied.

"Rumor travels faster, but it doesn't stay put as long as truth."
– Will Rogers

Chapter Twelve

It was early October and there was a seasonal chill in the air. I enjoyed my drive into the office but was beginning to feel some anxiety about Jake's family and what the FBI referred to as 'an impending visit'. I had hardly poured my coffee and sat down at my desk when Agent Stephens called.

"Good morning, Sheriff."

"It is going to be a cool one today," I replied.

"Sheriff, I will get to the point. The Feds are having a hard time nailing down the timing of the King family's visit, but they remain confident they are coming. They are thinking sooner rather than later. The good news is that if they leave the Tremont area, the FBI will be able to give you at least a few hours' notice before their arrival. That will give you time to do whatever is needed around your farm, and time for us to prepare."

I replied, "I would expect them soon. I am sure they understand it will not be long until all the leaves have fallen from the trees. That will make it harder for them to find and take cover."

"I think the FBI is in agreement with you on that. The only additional information I have is that the liquor store cashier is nowhere to be found. We do not know if he is in the wind, or if the family has done something with him. We would like to secure warrants and execute arrests for the three suspects who ambushed you and Deputy Allen, but the FBI continues building their case against them. They want as solid of a case as possible, and a statement from the cashier by itself is not sufficient for prosecution. The fact that he is missing hurts us."

I interrupted and asked, "The cashier is missing?"

"Yes sir. The FBI is actively looking for him. He is central to the case against the family. I think the Department of Conservation would like to spend some time with him as well regarding some potentially illegal trapping issues and the King clan."

"Do you think the family knew he talked to the FBI?"

"We do not know. But I can tell you the FBI is concerned about his availability moving forward. Regarding the family visiting your farm, the ideal scenario would be to prevent them from visiting your farm at all. But with the information the FBI has and the cashier's statements, we will be able to arrest them as soon as they step foot on your place. We will have enough to keep them in prison for a long time."

"Thanks, Agent Stephens. I appreciate the call and the information."

"If I hear anything else, I will come by your office or give you a call," he replied.

As we were ending our call, Beverly walked into the office and laid a note on my desk. It read, 'Doctor John called and asked that you stop by his office. Just tell the ladies at the front desk to send you back when you arrive.'

I walked down the hall to Shelley's office and provided a King family update for her. Her concern for the children was clearly evident in her facial expression.

"Will, are you comfortable that the FBI will be able to give us sufficient warning and time to prepare for them?"

"Yes. Agent Stephens assured me the FBI would know when the family members left Tremont. That gives us a solid estimated arrival time. That is if they drive straight to the farm. If not, the FBI will be surveilling them anyway. They hope to make arrests when the family members arrive at the farm. If they are armed that gives them 'conspiracy' and is sufficient to make arrests. If they actually start shooting, that puts them away for a long, long time."

After returning to my office, I struggled to maintain focus on the events of the day. Knowing that someone wants to kill you forces other thoughts from your mind. As I was walking the hall to leave the courthouse for the day, I noticed Steph McGee walking down the hallway. It appeared that he was leaving CPS and was on his way out of the building.

I stopped him and commented that we needed to talk. I asked him to come back to the office with me.

As I closed the door behind him, I commented, "Shelley Corntassel tells me you have been following her around town. She commented that you followed her while she was driving home a couple of evenings ago. I told her it must be a coincidence. There is no way you would try to intimidate an employee of Child Protective Services. Especially since they have temporary custody of your son while they investigate his home situation and concern over domestic violence. That would not be a smart thing to do."

"I am free to drive wherever I want whenever I want," he replied.

"Yes, technically you are. But in Carlin County, CPS employees are officers of the court. If you do something that is perceived as harassing or threatening to an officer of the court, you may be arrested and jailed. When it involves someone close to me, it will lead to an additional response. One that is a lot more painful and embarrassing than the one of a legal nature."

"Are you threatening me?" he asked.

"Just to be clear and ensure there is no confusion, yes. To avoid any legal issues as interim sheriff, I can take off this badge and resign my position. I will do that in a heartbeat if she sees you following her again."

Shortly after McGee left my office, Deputy Kingfisher knocked on my door and entered.

"Sheriff, I overheard a bit of your conversation and wanted to let you know that McGee is one of ours."

"What do you mean one of ours?" I asked.

"He works with us."

"What do you mean he works with us? That man is not on the payroll."

"He is a CI. A snitch."

"What is CI?" I asked.

"A confidential informant," Kingfisher replied.

"Are you saying I need to give him a pass? What are you saying?"

"No sir. That is not what I am saying. I just wanted you to know that he works with us."

I asked, "So, we have something on him that he is avoiding consequences for?"

"Yes sir."

"Since CPS is holding his son, tell me it is not a domestic violence issue."

Kingfisher replied, "It is not domestic violence. We are sitting on a petty disturbing the peace charge, but he cannot afford any legal attention due to probation status."

"How many of these CIs do we have?" I asked.

"Well, they come and go, but typically we have four to five that let us know things that are going on in the county. They do not get a pass on serious matters, but they may earn some latitude for misdemeanors or minor incidents. We try to keep a couple in our pocket to keep us abreast of what is happening around the bars, and a couple to let us know what is going on in the drug arena."

"That is something Joe did not tell me. Bring me a list of who we currently have as CIs and make sure I know when that list changes."

I could not imagine what Doctor John wanted to discuss with me, but I decided to make a brief stop by his office on the way home. As instructed, I told the lady at the front desk that Doctor John had said to send me back and let him know I had arrived. She escorted me to his office and directed me to wait. She commented, "I will let him know you are here. He should be with you in just a minute."

It was only a few moments later that Doctor John entered his office and closed the door. "I will get right to the point. I treated a man recently and put a couple of stitches on his lip. While I was treating him, he commented that he received his injury from you."

"Doc, you have to understand…"

He interrupted, and continued, "I neither need to know nor want to know what happened. That is your business. I have known you for a long time and I figure if you did that, he probably deserved it."

I replied, "I can only assume I know who the fellow was, but you can safely assume he either took a swing at me or took a swing at someone inside his home. Neither of those acts will go without a harsh response from me."

"You mean there is more than one?" he asked. "Again, I do not need to know. I just want to tell you that if he is talking to me, he is probably telling others. I do not want to see you get yourself into trouble. That is all I needed. Stop by and get a checkup sometime. It has been too long."

It had been a long day and I was happy to be home and have family around me. I tried to ensure I never took the job home with me, but this cloud over me was unrelenting. The kids knew I was the interim sheriff, and occasionally saw me that way, but I tried to be Dad or Will when at home. However, the ongoing issue with the King family made separating the two roles difficult. With the uncertainty of the timing of the King family's visit, I had to be the interim sheriff at home as well.

During dinner that evening Shelley and I discussed the King family issue with the kids.

I explained, "A man named Jake Cummings and I were neighbors and went to school together, and at times had been friends. We'd had some minor issues in our past, but never anything significant until James and Jenni's mom was the victim of a homicide. Sheriff Joe and I believed that Jake Cummings was the person who killed their mom. Eventually, Jake Cummings was shot by county deputies, and he died."

Shelley added, "He was a very violent man and had been in prison many times for violent acts against people."

Mary asked, "Why are you telling us this?"

I replied, "We are telling you this because Jake Cummings' family thinks I had something to do with his death and has threatened to come to the farm and try to hurt me."

Shelley explained, "We need you to be alert when you are away from the house. If you see anything or anybody suspicious, you let us know immediately. If you see a stranger on the farm, let us know."

I added, "We have no reason to think they want to harm any of you, but you must be alert. Do you understand?"

They all replied, "Yes Sir."

Shelley commented, "If you have questions or are scared, just come talk to us. We will not let anything happen to you. If they try to come to the house, the FBI will know, and they will tell us. We will leave and go to a safe place until they are gone."

I added, "We cannot stress enough, if you have questions let us know. If you see something let us know."

"Are you okay?" Shelley asked.

"Yes Ma'am," they replied.

"Do the best you can, and don't take life too serious."
– Will Rogers

Chapter Thirteen

Shelley and I took advantage of the fact that both of us worked in the courthouse, and frequently enjoyed having lunch together. During one of our lunch visits, I saw Bruce sitting at his usual table. I walked over, shook his hand, and said, "Bruce, it has been a while."

"Yes, sheriff, it has been too long. When you have some time, you should stop by the office."

"I agree. Are you busy this afternoon? I asked.

"I know I have nothing after lunch. Stop by around one o'clock if you can."

"I will see you then," I affirmed.

As I entered Bruce's office, he commented, "Sheriff, I may have told you before, but I have never met a man who works as hard as you do. It seems you never stop. Do you ever sleep?"

"Oh, I assure you I do not work all the time. I can see where it might look that way though. But I will not back down from a day of hard work."

"Yeah, it certainly looks that way."

I commented, "I noticed a new award hanging on the wall when I walked into your office. What is that?"

Demonstrating his typical humility, he replied, "Oh, it is just a little thing from the university."

I walked over to the framed certificate and read parts out loud. "For outstanding service to The University of Tulsa. It says you have been recognized as an outstanding educator for your years of service in the Law School. I may not be an educated man, but it does not look like a little thing to me."

"That all happened a long time ago," he replied.

I commented, "Like we said, it has been too long since we spoke. I realized today that I have never thanked you for all you did for me during my training to assume this role. I want you to know I appreciate what you did for me then, and all you have done for me over the past twenty-five years."

I continued, "Before he passed away, my grandfather told me to find that thing in life that you are good at that makes your heart beat, the thing that makes you feel alive. Share that one thing and make someone's life better, even if it is temporary comfort or a moment of laughter. You may search your entire life for that thing, but never stop searching. He explained that it was only when he was older, he realized his purpose seemed to be sharing the values and things he had learned growing up as a Cherokee. The thousands of years of native history carried lots of stories and bits of wisdom. For him, sharing those things became his purpose."

I added, "Being an attorney seems to have been your calling. It is something you do well and seem to be content with."

Bruce replied, "I have never thought of it quite that way or in those terms, but I would say that is correct. I think this is what I was meant to do. I hope I have helped people."

He continued, "Will, I have always enjoyed your stories of your grandfather. Over the past twenty-plus years, you have shared many of his stories and bits of wisdom. I have always learned something from their message."

"Thanks, Bruce. I appreciate that. Sometimes I feel that folks get tired of hearing my stories."

"Never," he replied.

As it begins to ring, I pull my cell phone from my pocket. "Well Bruce, it looks like I am back to work." I shook his hand and began walking back to my office.

"Hey Beverly, what is going on?" I asked.

"You asked to meet with Deputy Carter when she was available. Are you anywhere near the office," she asked.

"I am on my way from Bruce's office. I will be there in a minute."

"Okay, I will let her know you are on your way."

Deputy Carter met me at Beverly's desk and we walked to my office. As we entered the office I closed the door behind her.

"What do you need sheriff?" she asked.

"Have a seat. I want to update you on the FBI and OSBI investigation. One issue is that the FBI is confident the King family is going to pay me a visit at the farm."

"Seriously, they plan to come to your home?"

"It appears that way. The second item is the liquor store cashier is missing."

She asked, "Do they think the family did something to him?"

"They do not know."

After sitting quietly for a moment, I looked at Carter and commented, "Had Deputy Watts not called in with a family issue the evening of the liquor store robbery, I would have never gone to the liquor store. I would have been off duty. I would have been…"

Deputy Carter interrupted me and asked, "How did they know you were on duty? Do you think somebody tipped them off?"

I replied, "Yes, I do. Otherwise, they would have never had the opportunity to get me in the liquor store."

"But who was it? Who would do that?" she asked. "It would not be anybody from our department."

I explained, "Either somebody told them I was on duty, or somebody created the situation where I would be on duty for the evening. For someone to call and tell them I was on duty would make no sense. They would not have known they would be able to get me into the store that evening until I held over. That would make the timing very difficult."

"So, they knew before that day that you would be on the evening shift," she commented.

"Yes. Someone had to create the situation that required me to hold over."

She asked, "You think Watts was involved? You asked me to think about why county dispatch was called and not city dispatch. I could make no sense of it until now. They wanted to isolate you."

I asked, "During your investigation, did you confirm who made the robbery call to the dispatcher?"

"No, I did not."

"Okay, I cannot express how important it is to keep this between you and me, but I need you to investigate one of our own. Are you comfortable doing that?"

"Yes sir. If Watts set you up for that, I will hound dog him until I prove it. I have never dreamed that anybody I work with would be dirty."

"Obviously, you need to be very careful. If you uncover something that needs to be investigated, we will ask Director Simmons to assign an agent to do the follow-up."

"You can count on me, sheriff. That pisses me off."

"Be diligent and thorough but be careful. Let's talk every couple of days. Thanks, Carter. I knew you were the deputy I could turn to."

*"If stupidity got us in this mess,
how come it can't get us out."*
— **Will Rogers**

Chapter Fourteen

The call I had been dreading came early on Saturday afternoon. "Sheriff Rogers, this is Agent Stephens. We just received notice from the FBI that four King family vehicles have left Tremont and are now westbound on Interstate 44. There are two people in each vehicle for a total of eight. We have descriptions of all four vehicles. If they drive directly to your farm, they should be there around sunset, but we expect them to wait until it is dark before coming to your farm. We have three agents en route and the FBI has four agents en route from their Tulsa office. Two FBI agents who have been working in the Tremont area are in the air and will meet with OSBI and FBI agents at three o'clock at your farm. If you can have your deputies there, that would be good. We should have a total of ten to twelve agents plus you and any deputies you assign. We will need to park our vehicles in your barn unless you have another location that will keep them out of sight."

"I will have deputies here at three o'clock. Depending on how many vehicles there are, there should be room to park them in the barn. I will close the doors. Nobody will be able to see them in the barn."

Agent Stephens continued, "Mark Gheen is the FBI Agent in Charge. He will give an update and present the plan for the King family's arrival. The FBI will bring and deploy drones. The drones will be equipped with night vision and infrared technology. As soon as the King family members are in place to execute an attack and we see weapons, we will begin making arrests."

Following Agent Stephen's update, I called the county Dispatcher and requested she call out three deputies at two o'clock for the overnight shift. Deputy Carter will explain the evening's activities when they arrive at the courthouse for duty.

I then called Deputy Carter. "What do you need sheriff," she asked.

I explained the plan for the evening. "Without disclosing to the deputies what is going on, I need you to have them follow you to my farm. When you get to the farm, we will receive an update from the FBI. I need you to have Watts ride with you. I need you to keep an eye on him,"

"Yes sir, I will do that."

"From the time he reports for duty, do not let him out of your sight. He cannot make any calls or send any texts."

I immediately turned to Shelley and discussed the update. "You will have time to take the kids to the courthouse. This should be over quickly, but we do not know what time they will arrive."

She replied, "I would never want to put the kids in any danger. I can take them and come back. I do not like the idea of leaving you here alone."

"I will not be alone. There will be at least a dozen other law enforcement officers here with me. Pack some things for the kids to do and take them to the courthouse. Even the King family will not be inclined to break into jail."

"I can take the kids to my parents and come back here."

"No, your parents' place is too predictable."

"Will, I am not leaving here without you. I will take a shotgun and go to the spring. But I am not leaving you."

"Shelley, you cannot be here. Not only am I against it, the OSBI and FBI will demand you leave."

At three o'clock, The FBI began the update. During the update, FBI agent Gheen commented they just received word that three of the vehicles exited the interstate and were traveling southbound on Highway 43 in Missouri. The fourth vehicle is continuing westbound toward Tulsa.

During the update, Agent Gheen added that since they were expecting King family members to scatter in the woods, all deputies and agents would stage along the creek, by the barn, and by the well house.

With a creek thirty yards to the south of the house, a steep hillside and timber to the west, and open pasture to the north, an approach from the east was the most logical. The east side of the house is the front lawn, bordered by timber. Due to it being the closest area that allows cover, it was assumed the family would take cover and approach from the timber east of the house. The thing that virtually ensured this approach was the location of the county road. The road ran north to south along the back of the timber east of the house. That would provide the shortest distance of travel for family members to get to the house and the shortest distance in the event of a retreat. Staging agents in a line running north to south was smart planning by the FBI. We would maintain a wide defensive position whether the family approached from the east or the west. Since it appeared the family was bringing six members, it would also be easy to maintain both left and right flanks.

Following the FBI debrief, I gathered all county deputies together. I explained, "We do not want to lose our advantage this evening because of a call or text, so I need everybody's cell phone. We cannot have a phone light up or go off and give away the element of surprise or give away someone's position." I collected all the phones and placed them in a small box inside the house.

I called Deputy Carter to the side and explained what I needed her and the three other deputies to do and reminded her to not let Watts out of her sight. I informed Agent Gheen that since it appeared only six family members were coming to the farm and we should have enough agents posted, I would utilize my deputies elsewhere, as a secondary resource. He agreed.

I told Shelley to take the kids to the courthouse and remain with them. I explained this would not take too long and that Deputy Edmonds would be with them. He had instructions to lock them down where they could not be reached. Shelley and the kids left within moments. She was carrying a 12 gauge shotgun with a box of shells in the car with her.

As the sun began to set over the ridge to the west and the long afternoon shadows faded, the plan was put into motion. FBI agents staged the drones outside the barn. Two agents remained in the barn to operate the drones, providing field direction for all law enforcement. One FBI agent staged by the road to the west, and another staged by the road to the east. After the King family vehicles passed by them, the agents would join the right and left flanks with the rest of the agents.

One of the FBI agents radioed and notified us the fourth vehicle had exited the interstate and appeared to be en route to Shelley's parents' home. The OSBI directed two agents in Tulsa to relocate there.

I went through the house and turned on a few lights to make it appear there were people in the house. If needed, I would cycle a couple of lights off and on to add realism. I took my place underneath the largest window in our living room. Although it drew some odd looks from FBI and OSBI agents, I had fabricated a decoy to draw fire from the King family. It was a broom handle with a shirt and hanger taped to the end. I intended to pass it in front of the window to draw gunfire. It was at the ready.

When everyone was in place, the drones were launched and confirmed that all agents were accounted for. The drones returned to the barn.

It was approximately 7:15 p.m. when the agent posted by the road west of the farm radioed that two suspect vehicles had passed his location. Only a couple minutes later, the agent to the east radioed that one suspect vehicle had passed their post.

From the barn, a notification went out to be ready. As soon as it was verified the family members had exited their vehicles and were on foot, the drones would be launched, and their numbers and positions would be provided.

I knew it would take the family members a few minutes to get close enough to the house to engage me, so I lay on the floor and listened to the radio traffic.

The drones were in the air, and I was surprised at the speed of reporting. Six family members were accounted for as well as their location and distance relative to the timber line. The communication from the barn continued as the family made their way closer and closer to the house. I decided it would be a good time to turn off the kitchen light and turn on the lights in the dining and living rooms. I returned to my post underneath the living room window. One suspect continued making their way toward the barn, which was now guarded by numerous agents, as well as the agent previously posted by the road to the west.

Eventually, communication from the barn that all family members except the one by the barn had stopped moving and were positioned in a line just inside the edge of the timber. We had both flanks and a defensive line from the creek to the north of the barn. We were ready for whatever came.

I radioed that I would move my decoy to cast a shadow and see if it drew fire. As I moved it from the left side of the window to the right, a volley of shots pierced the window. I was showered with broken glass. We now had all we needed for charges against the family. I turned off all lights as I raced through the house, exited through the back door, and joined the OSBI and FBI agents outside. Sporadic gunfire continued. I communicated that I was going to disable their vehicles and began a broad swing to the south side of the property. I crawled along the creek bank until I knew I was past where they were positioned in the timber. I rose to my feet and began running. The three vehicles were parked in various positions and locations along the edge of the road. I plunged the blade of my knife through the sidewall of the tires on all three vehicles and returned to a flank position south of the timber. Once I had returned, agents were free to return fire if needed.

Next was a thing of beauty that I did not know would happen. The drones, with high-intensity LED lights, lit up the edge of the timber. Agent Gheen, over a loudspeaker, announced their presence and notified the family to drop their weapons and exit the timber with their hands behind their heads. None did, but agents could see the family members beginning a retreat. They were allowed to retreat deeper into the timber. The family member who had positioned himself near the barn began running north. An FBI agent began foot pursuit of him. He was captured and cuffed within a couple hundred yards. As the suspects continued their retreat, lights on the drones were turned off and field agents were again being guided by the agents in the barn. The agents formed a line and entered the timber cautiously. I suspected we all knew the family was working their way back to their vehicles. The Carlin County surprise was that the road to the east and west was now blocked by my deputies. Even if the family tried to drive on flat tires, they were not going to get past the roadblocks. There were two deputies located alongside the road in each location in a position that would place them behind a vehicle stopping at the roadblocks. That positioning might only provide a temporary advantage, but it was an advantage.

As anticipated, family members attempted an escape with their vehicles. One vehicle traveled east and two traveled west. I was sure it was hard to control the vehicles on the road, but they did manage to get to the roadblocks. As the FBI and OSBI agents had continued following the family's retreat into the timber, two FBI agents returned to the barn and were now driving FBI vehicles. So, shortly after the suspect vehicles approached the roadblocks, the agents' vehicles rolled in behind them blocking any possible escape. At the east roadblock, the two family members exited their vehicle with guns drawn. As Deputy Ridge gave the command for them to drop their weapons, one suspect turned toward him with his handgun in hand. He was dispatched immediately.

That was the only shot fired by law enforcement. The remaining family members surrendered without further incident. An immediate call was issued for an ambulance, which Deputy Carter had dispatched and staged a bit further down the road.

After all suspects were removed and en route to jail, I called Shelley and told her the excitement was over. "They are on their way to county lockup."

She was emotional. With her voice quivering, she said, "Deputy Edmonds had the radio in the other room and I could hear gunfire. I was imagining the worst."

It did not help when I told her all of the shots she heard were them shooting at me in the house.

She continued, "Then minutes later I heard an ambulance siren. I was afraid for you."

"I am fine. I will be fine." I asked Shelley, "Do you want to take the kids and get a room in town? The house is not a good place to be tonight, and I do not want you going to your house. It is going to be a long night at the courthouse, especially since Deputy Ridge shot one of them. The paramedics said the guy he shot would survive, but Deputy Ridge has some things we will have to go through. There will be two FBI agents at the house through the night in case the family plans a second wave. The FBI has not heard any chatter about that, but we want to be sure. We will need to replace the living room window. We will have to see what other damage there is tomorrow."

We worked well into the night completing reports and documenting Deputy Ridge's use of force and discharging his weapon. Agents from the FBI and OSBI searched for hours for the two family members who had appeared to be en route to Shelley's parents' house. Although they had not been located, we had plans for the remaining six family members and were diligently making lodging arrangements for them. After discussing with the OSBI and FBI, they agreed we should keep the six family members separated. To do that we had to transport two of them to the Fain County jail.

The following day was surreal. My farm had once again been the site of the ultimate act of violence – an attempt to end a person's life. Particularly troubling was the fact that it was my life they wanted to end. The damage from the gunfire was not limited to the window, but only minor repairs would be needed.

After returning home, Shelley picked up and was holding the crude decoy I had fabricated. There was a bullet hole clearly visible through one of the pockets. As she pointed at the hole, she commented, "I hope this is not what I am thinking it is."

"Ouch! That would have hurt," I said to her.

"Don't make jokes about it. That could have been you."

"At least they shot the right dummy. He had a short life, but he served his purpose," I replied with a smile.

FBI and OSBI agents spent the morning searching the timber for shell casings, weapons, or any other evidence left by the family.

Shelley and I worked with a neighbor and a couple of my deputies to clean up the glass and debris from the night before, and we boarded up the window. Additional minor repairs would be required, but the house was fit for humans to live in again.

We spent the remainder of the day relaxing and putting a little effort into mental recovery from recent events.

Late in the afternoon, Director Simmons called. "Will, we had a successful close to the investigation and are planning to have a celebratory drink this evening at the watering hole out by the bridge west of town. We hope you can meet us for a drink. We will be returning home early tomorrow morning."

I thanked him for the invitation but told him I would not be able to attend. I explained, "I know the bar you are going to. It is a place that many locals and tourists enjoy when they are looking for a fun place to have a drink. You should enjoy your time there. But there is a demon in the bar that knows my name. He cannot come outside the bar, and I cannot go inside. We just leave it that way."

"Sheriff, I admit when you pulled out the broom handle with a shirt taped to it, I had some doubts about what you were doing. It was unorthodox, but it worked out better than I could have dreamed."

"Thanks," I said with a chuckle. "One thing I learned growing up around firearms is that when a person carries a gun, they have a strong desire to discharge it… they want to shoot something. I just figured we should take advantage of that."

"When you requested to use your deputies as secondary resources, we had no idea you were setting up roadblocks… and staging an ambulance. What made you think of that?" he asked.

"I was concerned about folks driving down the county road if there was an exchange of gunfire. And I knew we had numbers on them and would win a gun battle. Eventually, their only option would be to retreat. And I certainly did not want them to escape. If they escaped, I would have to deal with them again, and I am tired of dealing with them. My hope is that I am finally free from the curse of having known Jake Cummings.

"It was a smart maneuver. You know, you might be pretty good at this sheriff thing."

I replied, "Thank you. I kind of like this job and I hope to find my feet someday."

He commented, "One last thing for now, the FBI has assigned resources to continue the search for the two family members who eluded us. They will find them."

They were not located until their return to the Tremont area. Unfortunately, the two would never be charged. They did not commit a crime in Oklahoma, and the FBI did not have sufficient evidence to charge them for their involvement in the conspiracy to kill me.

At some time around four o'clock Shelley and I decided to take a walk through the timber. It was a cool day with a slight breeze from the northwest. We walked along quietly holding hands. Eventually, I broke the silence. "You know I have grown to love you and the girls. I know it has only been four months that we have been seeing each other, but the heart wants what the heart wants. The heart does not know the calendar. It knows emotion. I am letting you know that I do not see myself here or anywhere else without you and the girls."

"We have grown to consider you, James, and Jenni as family as well," she replied.

I drew a deep breath and told her, "I had a thought the other day that illustrates my feelings:"

'If I lost my memory today and could not recall my name.
If I lost my memory today and everyone looked the same,
I would still remember how lucky I have been to love you.'

"Will Rogers, you never stop surprising me. I did not know you were such a romantic man. Those are quite possibly the kindest words ever spoken to me."

"It is funny, the words have always been in my mind and in my heart, but I have never been able to speak them out loud until now. I have told you before that being with you is different. That is what I mean when I say it is different. I am different."

Shelley replied, "Whether it has been months or years is not important. I enjoy the way my heart beats when I see you. It makes me feel like that little girl with a crush on you again. When I see you, I wait to hear your voice. It comforts me and I know I am protected. I am safe. My girls are safe."

I told her, "If someone had asked me a few years ago, I would have said I was a very happy man. I was pleased with my life and found comfort and joy in the things I did and the friends I had. Now I look back and realize I was just living, finding comfort in my routine. I was living an unfulfilling life that benefitted nobody. Maybe I had been fooling myself."

I continued, "Today I have something to look forward to when I come home. There is joy and laughter there. I am learning to do a job I enjoy with people I admire and respect. I have an opportunity to do things to help others have a better life. I can make a difference instead of living a self-centered empty life dictated by the mundane comfort of routines."

I explained, "You and I make sense. You hold the key that unlocks my future and prevents me from returning to an unremarkable life of mediocrity. You lift my spirit to do something meaningful. Do not cast me back to a life that benefits nobody. Stay by my side."

"All I know is just what I read in the papers, and that's an alibi for my ignorance."
– Will Rogers

www.ingramcontent.com/pod-product-compliance
Lightning Source LLC
LaVergne TN
LVHW010215070526
838199LV00062B/4591